Actively Seeking Inc

Studies in Inclusive Education Series

Series Editor: Roger Slee, Dean of the Graduate School of Education, University of Western Australia

Actively Seeking Inclusion: Pupils with Special Needs in Mainstream Schools
Julie Allan

Actively Seeking Inclusion:
Pupils with Special Needs in Mainstream Schools

Julie Allan

UK   Falmer Press, 1 Gunpowder Square, London, EC4A 3DE

USA   Falmer Press, Taylor & Francis Inc., 325 Chestnut Street, 8th Floor, Philadelphia, PA 19106

First published in 1999

A catalogue record for this book is available from the British Library

ISBN 0 7507 0737 2 cased
ISBN 0 7507 0736 4 paper

Library of Congress Cataloging-in-Publication Data are available on request

Jacket design by Caroline Archer

Typeset in 10/12pt Times by
Graphicraft Limited, Hong Kong

Printed in Great Britain by Biddles Ltd., Guildford and King's Lynn on paper which has a specified pH value on final paper manufacture of not less than 7.5 and is therefore 'acid free'.

Every effort has been made to contact copyright holders for their permission to reprint material in this book. The publishers would be grateful to hear from any copyright holder who is not here acknowledged and will undertake to rectify any errors or omissions in future editions of this book.

Contents

A very short space of time through very short times of space. Five, six: the *nacheinander*. Exactly: and that is the ineluctable modality of the audible. Open your eyes.

James Joyce, *Ulysses*

Reproduced with the kind permission of the Estate of James Joyce.

Acknowledgments

Some previously published work has been developed in this book and I would like to acknowledge the journals and publishers concerned. These are: 'Foucault and special educational needs: A "box of tools" for analysing children's experiences of mainstreaming', *Disability and Society*, **11**, (2) 1996, pp. 219–33; 'With a little help from my friends? Integration and the role of mainstream pupils', *Children and Society*, **1**, (3) 1999, pp. 183–93; 'I don't need this: Acts of transgression by students with special educational needs', in Ballard, K. (ed.) (1999) *Inclusive Education: International Voices on Disability and Justice*, London, Falmer Press; 'Theorising special education inside the classroom: A Foucauldian analysis of pupils' discourses', in Haug, P. and Tøssebro, J. (eds) (1998) *Theoretical Perspectives on Special Education*, Kristiansand, Norwegian Academic Press. Thanks go to a number of people who provided encouragement and/or critical comment on the book. In particular, I would like to thank Ian Stronach who has supported this work from the beginning and has been instrumental in its development. I am also grateful to members of the International Inclusion Colloquium and to Roger Slee, the series editor. My warmest appreciation is reserved for the 11 young people who feature in this book. They and their mainstream peers spoke to me with wit and candour, taught me how to listen and helped me to see what was possible.

Series Editor's Preface

Julie Allan has responded to the political challenge of *voice* in studies in inclusive education. Allan is among the rising number of '. . . scholars [who] have interrupted the membrane of objectivity across the academy and in their respective disciplines, refusing containment and asking how feminist [disability] politics can and do play, explicitly and subversively, in our lives' (Fine, 1994: 14). She moves directly to the ontological heart to interrogate how we frame knowledge about disability and education, and what various forms of knowledge do to both the 'knower' and their subject. 'The power that loiters between' (Fine, 1994: 14) the researcher and the research subjects is itself seized within the analytic gaze, rendered problematic and politicized.

Throughout the text one is moved by her sense of the researcher as a cultural worker engaged in teaching transgressions (hooks, 1994). Transgression is central to the work of this text as we are invited to listen to non-disabled and disabled students' discourses and observe the complex regimes of inclusion and exclusion colluding and colliding with each other in the school. Carefully explicating governmentality through pastoral power and pedagogic strategy, we witness the 'broadly positive and supportive' discourses of schools and non-disabled students, and 'at times highly punitive' exclusion of disabled students by non-disabled students and teachers. Particularly important in this study is the meticulous portrayal of the transgressive strategies of disabled students that disrupt teachers' practices framed according to a discourse of 'need'.

Reaching 'critically, self-consciously and creatively rather than faithfully' into Foucault's (1997: 208) 'box of tools' this text achieves a sophisticated level of analysis that lends itself to a politics of hope for those engaged in the project of *imagining and reconstructing* (Friere and Shor, 1987: 185) special and, of course, regular education. What lies before you is not a descent into obfuscation to produce a clever and apolitical working of postmodernism played out in the site of disability research. Inclusion is an ethical project of 'actively shaping ourselves'. Allan presses us to examine the derivatives of our self-knowing, and the 'othering' that accompanies it, to reshape ourselves pursuant to the project of inclusion.

Julie Allan, along with Barry, Brian, Fiona, Graham, Laura, Peter, Phillip, Raschida, Sarah, Scott and Susan, has written a book that contributes to the evolving debate over theory in disability studies. The touchstones in the development of her theorizing are the voices of the disabled students, the insertions of disabled researchers and activists and her own interrogation of difference and identity. The effect is a respectful approach where the problematic of being a non-disabled researcher is recognized and explored as an issue of research politics. The representation of the students' voices is rich and enlivens the book.

In a field that is dominated by experts who know others and what they need *Actively Seeking Inclusion* is refreshing for its humility. I anticipate debate, even 'passionate' argument (if we accept the metaphor of desire, flesh and lovers invoked in the conclusion) to follow this publication. As the author asserts this is proper given the ongoing project of learning to respect difference and knowing how to undo our prevailing ineptitude in its presence.

References

FINE, M. (1994) 'Dis-tance and Other Stances: Negotiations of Power inside Feminist Research', in A. GITLIN (ed.) *Power and Method. Political Activism and Educational Research*, New York, Routledge.

FOUCAULT, M. (1977) 'Intellectuals and Power: a conversation between Michel Foucault and Giles Deleuze', in BOUCHARD, D. (ed.) *Language, counter-memory, practice: selected essays and interviews by Michel Foucault*, Oxford, Basil Blackwell.

FRIERE, P. and SHOR, I. (1987) *A Pedagogy for Liberation. Dialogues on Transforming Education*, Basingstoke, Macmillan.

HOOKS, B. (1994) *Teaching to Transgress. Education as the Practice of Freedom*, New York, Routledge.

Introduction

This book is about 11 pupils with special needs, who were actively seeking inclusion in mainstream schools. The voices of the pupils and their mainstream peers are foregrounded and read alongside those of other interested parties — teachers, other professionals and parents — as well as the more formal discourses of special needs. The pupils' accounts, thus, are not essentialized and treated as indicative of how things *really* are, but are viewed as part of a complex power/knowledge knot, which is not supposed to be unravelled (Simons, 1995). Research on the mainstreaming of children with special needs has tended to concentrate on the amount of integration taking place, seldom moving beyond crude notions of how much time a child spends in an ordinary school or classroom or 'inventories of human and physical resources' (Slee, 1993: 351). The technical and empiricist bases of knowledge production and the 'methodological individualism' of researchers (Oliver, 1992a: 107) has had the effect of constructing children with special needs as objects on whom this knowledge is exercised. The voice of the child is absent from most accounts of special education, silenced by professional discourses of needs which are concerned with matters of placement or practice:

> Despite the growth of the disability movement and the struggles of disabled people
> to control the decision-making processes which shape their lives, little attention
> has been given to the say that young people have in controlling their education . . .
> They are the recipients (or not) of other people's decisions. (Swain, 1993: 156)

Where their voices have been foregrounded (Lewis, 1994; Lynas, 1986a; Sheldon, 1991) these have been read either positivistically, connecting truths to objects outside of language, or phenomenologically, connecting truth to the consciousness of individual knowers (Ligget, 1988). Research by Armstrong, Galloway and Tomlinson (1993) on the assessment experiences of pupils with emotional or behavioural difficulties and their exclusion from the assessment process by professionals is a notable exception. Such work reinforces the importance of examining pupils' perspectives in the context of the power/knowledge relationships in which they were obtained.

The discursive regimes of the pupils were full of oscillations, uncertainties and ambivalences, which disturb the binarism usually associated with special needs (for example included/excluded; normal/special; able-bodied/disabled) and which constructs individuals as 'the other half of an undesirable pair' (Marks, 1994: 73). The pupils' accounts evoke a space in the relationship between self and other, a kind of two way gaze, 'with the figure of authority turning its gaze on the victim and the victim looking back' (MacCannell and MacCannell, 1993: 214). This suggests the impossibility of locating pupils permanently at one or other end of these polarities, for example as either included or excluded, since most of the action occurs in 'the disturbing-distance-in-between' (Bhabha, 1994: 45) the binary divisions.

Children have the right to be informed and listened to on all matters affecting them (Clelland and Sutherland, 1996; United Nations, 1989). As Alderson and Goodey argue, however, creating ethical research standards that respect children's worth and dignity requires a more fundamental consideration of power, stereotyping and children's status. Anxieties about researching children can lead to 'perceiving, constructing and reporting them as a different species' (1996: 108). Where children with special needs are concerned, researchers risk misconstruing data by analysing it within developmental frameworks or around constructs of competence (Gerber, 1990). Booth and Booth (1996) have reported problems associated with interviewing individuals with learning difficulties, for example, inarticulateness, unresponsiveness and difficulties with the concept of time. The young people who took part in this research spoke with an ease and fluency which made the anticipation of any such problems misplaced and irrelevant. They were, quite simply, 'the best authority on their own lives, experiences and views' (Stalker, 1998: 5). Obtaining pupils' accounts was, however, highly challenging because of the ways in which their voices, and those of parents, have tended to be subordinated within a professional discourse. Teachers appeared uncomfortable with the status of pupils as active critics and the pupils expressed surprise to be placed in a situation where their views were central.

The Research

This research took place between 1992 and 1995 in mainstream schools in Scotland and formed the basis of a doctoral thesis (Allan, 1995). Pupils with special needs were interviewed individually and mainstream pupils were interviewed in groups. Break times provided informal opportunities to talk to the pupils, and their interaction in the classroom and playground was also observed. Permission to speak to mainstream pupils was sought from the pupils with special needs who were asked to suggest people to whom they were closest or who knew them well. Teachers were told that the views of pupils with special needs and mainstream pupils on integration were being sought confidentially, but this did not prevent them from assuming a right to be told what the pupils had said. The mainstream pupils were given the same information, with a great deal of emphasis placed on the value of their perspectives. They were told, for example, that they were 'the ones who really know what is going on in the school', implying an essentialist position which ran contrary to the research approach, but which was aimed at inciting the pupils to discourse.

Foucault's methodology or 'box of tools' (1977a: 208) was used to analyse both the official discourses on special needs and those operating within schools.

These discursive networks construct the pupils as passive subjects, tied to others through control and constraint and to their self-formed identities. Foucault argues that this infers a form of power which both 'subjugates and makes subject to' (1982: 212). He also urges us, however, 'to refuse what we are' (1982: 216), by struggling against subjectification. Thus, a Foucauldian perspective makes it possible to analyse ways in which pupils with special needs were constrained and how they resisted and contested the power that was exercised upon them.

The pupils' discourses revealed two complex regimes, which were both connected to, and distinctive from, other formal and informal regimes operating within the school (such as discipline or so-called 'peer pressure'). The first of these concerned the mainstream pupils and their mini-regime of 'governmentality' (Foucault, 1988a: 19). This had its own set of rules and features such as pastoral power and pedagogic strategies, and its effect was simultaneously to regulate and disrupt their conduct towards pupils with special needs. The mainstream pupils' governmental regime was broadly positive and supportive of pupils with special needs, but at times was highly punitive, legitimizing the exclusion of individuals. The second related to the pupils with special needs and their 'technologies of the self' (Foucault, 1988a: 18), transgressive practices which enabled them to resist attempts to label or exclude them and to seek alternative identities and experiences. The teachers' practices, framed within a discourse of 'needs', often challenged the pupils' transgressive practices where they appeared to disrupt the support they were trying to provide. As a consequence, pupils with special needs were forced to repeat acts of transgression in the space between the collusive and coercive markers provided by mainstream pupils and teachers. Thus, inclusion was never completed but was always in process.

Introducing the Pupils

The 11 pupils have been given pseudonyms and appear throughout the book either narrating their own stories or as part of other pupils', teachers' and occasionally their parents' accounts. They are listed here alphabetically, together with some information they or their friends revealed during our conversations.

- *Barry*, aged 12, attended a large mainstream primary school and was a wheelchair user. His twin brother went to the same school, but was in another class and his older brother was training to be a professional footballer. Barry was doing well at school and planned to become a teacher.
- *Brian*, also 12, was an only child with Down's Syndrome who attended his local primary. He was well known in his village and attended the local Boys' Brigade. He was going to a different secondary school from his classmates, because it had a special unit, but they looked forward to seeing him outside school.
- Fifteen-year-old *Fiona* described herself as tall, with brown hair, 'mad about horses' and deaf; her mainstream peers emphasized her 'horse mad'

characteristics. Her older brother was deaf and she had a hearing sister. Fiona was planning to leave school in the next year and — no surprises — to get a job working with horses.

- Sixteen-year-old *Graham's* interests lay in football and he attended matches regularly with his uncle, played snooker at home or went out with his older sister. He had not yet decided between a college course for students with learning difficulties and work when he left school, but thought he might prefer the latter.

- Fifteen-year-old *Laura*, the youngest of four in her family, was very bright and, according to one of her friends, 'funny' and 'quite wicked'. She attended a mainstream school, which provided specialist support for her visual impairment and intended to go to university, but had not yet selected a course.

- Twelve-year-old *Peter*, an only child, attended a rural primary school and split his time between mainstream classes and a special unit. He liked biking around the farm where he lived, hunting with his father and outdoor activities generally. He was looking forward to going to secondary school. He had been described as having emotional or behavioural difficulties.

- *Phillip*, 12, and the youngest of four in his family, was one of the cleverest in his class and a member of the school quiz team. His progressive condition in which his mobility was gradually decreasing had stopped him playing football, but he continued to enjoy watching it. He was not going to the same secondary school as most of his peers, because it had too many stairs, but some of his friends were going to be moving with him.

- Seventeen-year-old *Raschida* attended the same school as Laura and also shared the same 'wicked' sense of humour. She was the youngest of five children in her Muslim family and shared the same visual impairment as her two brothers. She was particularly good at maths and, although she had already been offered a place at University, was spending a sixth year improving her qualifications before selecting a course.

- *Sarah*, aged 12 and an only child, said that her favourite subject in secondary school was French and she had joined the French club. She also said she enjoyed school, although some of her mainstream peers drew attention to the bullying she had experienced because of her learning difficulties. She fancied becoming a nurse when she left school.

- *Scott*, also 12 and an only child, was a talented pianist, who could play pieces by Beethoven and Gershwin without the music. He played his own piano at home constantly and often spent his intervals playing the one in his mainstream primary school. He had a medical condition and learning difficulties.

- *Susan*, an 11-year-old only child, attended the same school as Peter and participated in both mainstream and special unit classes. She enjoyed going to school discos, but did not have many friends in the village where she lived. She had visited the Peto Institute in Hungary, which provides conductive education for children with cerebral palsy. She was looking forward to the different subjects in secondary school.

Perhaps the most striking thing about these mini-portraits was the incidental way in which their special needs appear. This is not contrived, nor is it intended to belittle their significance: as Raschida commented, 'I'd be a different person if I could see.' There were, however, far more interesting things which these young people revealed in conversation and I hope they will forgive my clumsy attempts to convey some of these without the promise of 'empathy' or 'authenticity' (Lather, 1998: 1) or 'unmediated access to the real' (Britzman, 1995: 235). They do, however, reflect a desire to highlight those characteristics and talents which tend to be overlooked by a dangerous assimilating gaze (Foucault, 1973a) which seeks out only the negative aspects of difference and forces children with special needs to experience 'social death' (Finkelstein, 1993a: 35).

Ten of the eleven pupils first appear in Chapter 3, as part of the mainstream pupils' accounts; Fiona appears later, in Chapter 7. In the dialogue between mainstream pupils, the first name initial is used to distinguish between different speakers, and I am referred to as JA. At the risk of interfering with the pupils' sharp dialogue, a small number of vernacular words or phrases have been replaced where their meaning might not be clear to non-Scots. The pupils' references to their schooling may need some explanation. In Scotland, they attend primary schools between the ages of 5 and 11 or 12 (referred to as primary 1–7) and secondary schools from 12 onwards. Some of the pupils in the research were taught in special units within their school as well as in mainstream.

The Structure of the Book

The book begins by examining the problems associated with research and theorizing in special needs and explores how these have contributed to a mythologizing of progress through discourses which have privileged certain 'truths' over others. There have been many calls over recent years for research in special education which is more sensitive to individuals' experiences (for example, Clough, 1995; Schindele, 1985) and Chapter 2 explores the contribution of a Foucauldian perspective to understanding the formal and informal special needs discourses which construct these experiences and identities. Chapter 3 focuses on mainstream pupils and examines the key role they played as 'gatekeepers' of inclusion, controlling the identities and experiences of the pupils with special needs within a mini-regime of governmentality (Foucault, 1988a). In Chapter 4, the transgressive practices of Raschida, Laura, Susan, Barry, Phillip and Peter are explored, using their own accounts and those of their peers. Chapter 5 turns to the teachers, whose practices, framed within a discourse of needs, often challenged the pupils' transgressive actions, articulated as desires rather than needs. Chapter 6 looks at how the semi-juridical process of opening and maintaining a Record of Needs (the Scottish equivalent of a statement) legitimized the professionals' gaze and allowed them to construct pupils and their parents as objects of their knowledge, highlighting needs while ignoring, or negating, the pupils' expressed desires. Chapter 7 focuses on Fiona, who, as a hearing impaired pupil, found herself neither fully a part of the deaf nor the hearing world and raises questions about the damaging consequences of inclusion where it is seen to equate with assimilation. This chapter also examines the collective transgression of the deaf community (using a lower case throughout, apart from direct quotations), which has demanded respect for deaf culture and values. Chapter 8 examines the silencing of the young people's gender and sexuality, their attempts to challenge this and other responses by disabled people to this form of oppression.

The final chapter takes its optimistic lead from the pupils with special needs, who have demonstrated their ability to be active subjects and challenge the identities and experiences given to them, and their mainstream peers, whose governmental regime was broadly supportive of inclusion. It establishes a framework of ethics (Foucault, 1987a) in which everyone — pupils, teachers, schools and researchers — has work to do on themselves in order to further the project of inclusion. At the same time, it seeks to avoid the promises of reconstruction of special education knowledge and even democracy offered by Skrtic (1995) or other kinds of rescue through, for example, the critical pedagogy of McLaren (1995). These are so ambivalent as to appear like 'an intellectual version of the hokey-cokey' (Stronach and Maclure, 1997: 19) and are unlikely to succeed. This chapter does, nevertheless, seek to urge everyone to 'know what they do . . . know why they do what they do . . . [and] know what they do does' (Foucault, cited in Dreyfus and Rabinow, 1982: 187). A Foucauldian study of special needs is not an exercise in gloom, since Foucault's point was not that 'everything is bad, but that everything is dangerous . . . If everything is dangerous, then we always have something to do' (1984a: 343). The ethical work we do on ourselves should enable us to shape our conduct according to how it will be experienced by others. If each of us recognizes the need for work of this kind, inclusion could become much more positive and creative, but not utopian, created both by and for everyone.

Chapter 1

Wandering Voices and Shifting Identities

Special education discourses function like rationalized myths about the actions taking place (Haug, 1998), and the positivistic orientation of researchers and the absence of rigorous theorizing about special education have served to reinforce certain 'truths' while negating others. One conviction has been that moves towards integration and inclusion represent significant progress and improvement in the lives of children with special needs. As a consequence of this mythologizing process, the schooling of pupils with special needs has been allowed to continue as 'a perverse form of prohibition in which desire as human agency is not permitted to explore its own constitutive possibilities' (McLaren, 1995: 233). This chapter begins by mapping out the discourses which shape special education, then examines the kind of research and theorizing about special needs which has taken place, questioning their contribution to understanding children's identities and experiences. It explores how the discourses of research have helped to mythologize a sense of progress in the education of pupils with special needs, helped to preserve the mystique of special education (Tomlinson, 1982) and enabled it to 'reinvent itself in order to stake its claim in the so-called era of inclusion' (Slee, 1998: 126). The failure of researchers to ask the right questions (or worse still their dogged determination to ask the wrong ones), their theoretical intransigence and their unwillingness to alter the social relations of research production is scrutinized. There are some grounds for optimism, however, and the chapter ends by exploring some of the more challenging critiques, theoretical perspectives and relations of research production, which may reverse the 'rip off' (Oliver, 1997: 15) which disabled people have been forced to endure.

Discourses that Shape Special Needs

Discourse is important because it 'worlds the world' (Lather, 1993: 675), framing the ways in which we know and act within contested spaces. Fulcher (1989) reminds us that discourses have uses rather than inherent meanings, that is, they serve particular interests, and Foucault argues that 'discourse may seem of little account, but the prohibitions to which it is subject reveal soon enough its links with desire and power' (1971: 11–12). Discourses also construct individuals as objects of particular kinds of knowledge: 'we do not speak the discourse. The discourse speaks us' (Ball, 1990a: 18). Medical, charity and rights discourses construct disabled peoples' identities and experiences, and Fulcher has suggested that lay and corporate discourses also have an important role in this process. Within educa-tion, a market discourse has emerged recently, shaping the experiences of teachers and pupils. A powerful new aesthetic discourse has been developed by disabled people; this particular discourse is discussed in the final chapter in the context of the work that disabled people have done on themselves. These discourses do not function independently of each other, but interact, often in a subversive way, making the construction of the identities and experiences of disabled people a com-plex and contradictory process.

Medical Discourse

A medical discourse defines individuals by their deficits, rather than by external factors (Fulcher, 1989; Sandow, 1993). It is criticized for being heavily patriarchal (Corbett, 1993) and dismissing disabled people under a single metaphysical category, which buries personalities (Brisenden, 1986). Fulcher (1989) suggests that medical discourse also individualizes disabilities as attributes and profession-alizes them by making them part of a person's technical trouble. Medical dis-course, through its language of 'body, patient, help need, cure, rehabilitation, and its politics that the doctor knows best' (Fulcher, 1989: 27) has dominated special educational practices (Tomlinson, 1982) and Oliver highlights the irony of the 'rehabilitation enterprise' (1996: 104). He suggests that the pursuit of walking and the restoration of the ability to walk is elevated to a millenarium movement in which walking is achieved by miraculous means (Abercrombie, Hill and Turner, 1988). Charities which support 'chronic and crippling diseases' (Oliver, 1996: 101) exist for the promotion of cures which are extremely rare. Oliver also suggests that the practice of conductive education on children with cerebral palsy could be likened to Nazism (1989). He contends that if able bodied children were removed from their communities, sent abroad and 'forced to undertake physical exercise for all their waking hours' (1996: 107), it would amount to child abuse and 'would rapidly come to the attention of the child protection mafia' (ibid.). As far as disabled children are concerned, however, 'anything goes as long as you call it therapeutic' (ibid.) and Oliver suggests that 'if it wasn't so sad it would be funny' (1989: 197). French warns against ignoring the experience of pain among disabled people while acknowledging that the routine linkage of disability with illness and disease has been 'extremely damaging' (1993: 19). Corbett (1993) argues for a reconstruction, rather than abandonment, of medical discourse, giving disabled people power over their own bodies and health care.

Charity Discourse

Within a charity discourse, disabled people become tragic figures who need help (Llewellyn, 1983), and Shapiro notes that individuals usually become defined either as objects of pity or sources of inspiration. He argues that both are oppressive, since they do not reflect the 'day-to-day reality of most disabled people, who struggle constantly with smaller challenges, such as finding a bus with a wheelchair lift' (1993: 17). Several writers (for example Goffman, 1963; Nietzsche, 1961; Sinason, 1992) have suggested that pity is a way of overcoming fear or guilt towards individuals or of masking aggression (Lacan, 1977). Morris describes her experience of the charity discourse as she experienced it, first from a doctor:

> I remember feeling outraged that the doctor who sat down at my bedside with a gloomy face, to tell me that I was permanently paralysed, should talk about how *tragic* it was. I felt that there was only one person who could say it was a tragedy and that was me — and I wasn't prepared to say that. (1991: 2, original emphasis)

and then from others, who began to see her as a source of inspiration:

> During the years following my accident, I have on countless occasions been told by both strangers and acquaintances how *wonderful* they think I am. It took a while to realise why this kind of remark provoked such anger in me. After all, those who say it seem to think that they are praising me for struggling against the difficulties which physical disability brings. When I eventually unpeeled the layers of patronising nonsense I realised that at the heart of such remarks lay the judgement that being disabled must be awful, indeed intolerable. It is very undermining to recognise that people look at me and see an existence, an experience, which they would do everything to avoid for themselves. (1991: 15, original emphasis)

Hevey invokes the 'tragedy principle' (1993: 116) to explain how the gaze of disability representation is a dynamic between the impaired body and social barriers. As a result, he argues, 'disablement means impairment and impairment means flaw' (1993: 117). The 'benevolent humanitarianism' (Tomlinson, 1982: 5) surrounding special education relates to both medical and charity discourses (Fulcher, 1989) and conceals the most selfish interests: '. . . whoever dreams of finding a fine situation for himself in the new schools never speaks of children without tears in his eyes. This is the everlasting comedy' (Binet and Simon, 1914: 10). The problem for special education, argues Tomlinson (ibid.), is that it is difficult to criticize.

Rights Discourse

A rights discourse, characterized by 'self reliance, independence, and consumer wants (rather than needs)' (Fulcher, 1989: 30) is explicitly political, although not always adversarial. Indeed, a rights discourse for some may reflect little more than discomfort over the unequal treatment of disabled people. The diversity within rights discourses, according to Oliver and Zarb (1989), undermines their political strength and disabled activists have called for greater solidarity within 'the movement' (Hasler, 1993: 284), suppressing difference in favour of 'marching to the beat of a single drum' (Shakespeare and Watson, 1997: 299). Organizations such as People First or Scope have set out to subvert medical and charity discourses and their negative portrayal of disabled people. As well as trying to educate the public, for example, through poster campaigns, some disabled rights activists have protested against charity events, such as Children in Need. Others, such as those involved in the campaign for a national disability income, have been more concerned with addressing material disadvantage. A rights discourse has as its theoretical basis the social model of disability, developed by disabled people.

Lay and Corporate Discourses

Fulcher (1989) specifies an additional lay discourse, which, she suggests, is informed by medical and charity discourses as well as fear and prejudice. Although this discourse may reveal some aspects of the stereotyping of disabled people, it appears to lack the depth offered by an analysis of medical and charity discourses. There is, however, a further discourse which Fulcher suggests is emerging and which appears central to the 'rules that constitute the meaning of disability' (Shapiro, 1981: 87). Fulcher refers to this as a corporate discourse, which is concerned with 'managing disability' (1981: 26). Within education, the most significant discourse to develop in the 1990s relates to marketization, in which special needs labels have been commodified and have become a key to additional resources.

Market Discourse

Riddell and Brown (1994) have observed how Warnock has entered the market place, extending the language of competition and choice to special needs and creating a climate of accountability which Ball refers to as the 'discourse of derision' (1990a: 18). Within this 'new discursive regime' (ibid.) the words spoken by professionals have been displaced by 'abstract mechanisms and technologies of *truth* and *rationality* — parental choice, the market, efficiency and management' (ibid., original emphasis). Barton (1993a; 1997) argues that government policies, such as the delegation of resources to schools, opting out and the publication of exam results undermine justice and equality by creating winners and losers and increasing the impetus for exclusion and segregation. One effect of this has been to reinforce perceptions of individual deficits and to encourage parents and teachers to seek formal acknowledgment of these, leading to a dramatic increase in requests for statements or Records of Needs (Evans et al., 1994; Riddell, Brown and Duffield, 1994). In an article in *The Guardian* (Berliner, 1993), Baroness Warnock confessed that she had been naïve not to anticipate that the system of statementing would be used in this way (Chapter 6). Armstrong and Galloway have noted a tendency of teachers to reconstruct children with emotional or behavioural difficulties as 'disturbed' (1994: 179), with the implication that these are outside the responsibilities of mainstream classroom teachers. Others have observed the 'epidemics' (Slee, 1996: 107) of Attention Deficit Hyperactivity Disorder and specific learning difficulties (Riddell et al., 1994; Clark et al., 1997). Slee suggests that the emergence of Attention Deficit Hyperactivity Disorder in Australia and the United States, is an effect of a 'disciplinary technology of surveillance and control' (1996: 108) to which children are willingly submitted by parents and teachers. The category provides respectability for parents — 'better to be seen as pathologically impaired than as bad' (ibid.) — and avoids difficult questions about pedagogy, curriculum and school organization for teachers. Slee argues, however, that pathologies should focus, not on individual children, but on schools and professional practices.

Research and the Myth of Progress

Researchers and commentators on special education have helped to sustain the myth of progress and reinforce the notion that 'disability is intrinsic to the child. Schools and teachers are not included in the diagnostic gaze' (Slee, 1996: 105). Skrtic (1995) points out that the functionalist orientation of knowledge production in special education reinforces assumptions about organizational rationality and individual pathologies, allowing school failure to be characterized as inherent in individuals. The view of special education as a euphemism for school failure (Barton, 1989; Slee, 1998) is obscured by researchers pursuing innocent knowing (Lather, 1996) of individuals and of the practice of special education upon them. The reductionist discourses of special educational research have focused on documenting the nature or causes of pupils' difficulties (Barton and Tomlinson, 1981) or in making integration or inclusion an 'actuarial quest' (Slee, 1996: 105), a mere matter of redistribution of resources. Barton and Tomlinson have criticized the descriptive nature of special education research for failing to examine critically the inherent assumptions and contradictions, which they argue are '. . . a product of complex social, economic and political considerations which may relate more to the *needs* of the wider society, the whole education system and professionals working within the system, rather than simply to the *needs* of individual children' (1984: 65, original emphasis). The needs of individuals, determined on the basis of professionals' logic of confidence (Meyer and Rowan, 1978; Skrtic, 1995), are privileged over their desires and interests, reducing pleasure to a concession or a diversion (Battaille, 1985).

There is agreement among many writers that the Warnock report (DES, 1978) represents a significant and positive watershed for special education (Gipps, Gross and Goldstein, 1987; Visser, 1993; Wedell, 1990). Hinson argues that the report brought 'beneficial consequences' (1991: 12), claiming that 'the cause of special education advanced steadily during the 1980s' (ibid.). Fish points to 'profound changes in thinking and practice' (1990: 219), precipitated by the Warnock report, that have not, however, 'been generally recognised and accepted' (ibid.). Fish also reflects on the importance of the Warnock report in reversing a trend which was 'outward' in the sense that special education provision was considered optimum. Warnock, he argues, was salutary in forcing the trend 'inward' and encouraging ordinary schools to meet special needs. Now, however, he suggests that 'limitations of all kinds placed on schools, together with increased expectations, may be expected to reverse the trend again . . . to an *outward* movement of children from primary and secondary schools' (Fish, 1990: 226–7, original emphasis).

The implications of this, he suggests, are serious, moving special education once again from the centre to the periphery. This outward movement could be read in Foucauldian terms as an example of 'dividing practices' (Rabinow, 1984: 8), similar to those which incarcerated lepers during the Middle Ages or confined the poor, the insane and vagabonds in a single hospital in the seventeenth century. Wedell argues that recent legislative and policy changes, such as the 1988 Education Act in England and Wales, have interrupted progress in understanding needs and making provision, casting 'a pall of doubt . . . as to whether the advances which have been achieved can be maintained, let alone furthered' (1990: 17).

Analysis of the failure to achieve the Warnock ideals has focused on technical or administrative problems arising from a lack of resourcing (Fletcher-Campbell with Hall, 1993; Lunt and Evans, 1994); a failure to adopt the 'whole school approach' (Clark et al., 1997: 34); the singular or collective inadequacies of teachers (Galloway and Goodwin, 1987; Hegarty, 1982) or a lack of commitment to integration (Booth, 1988). Implicit in each of these critiques is the notion that once these problems are resolved, progress can continue unabated. Yet, even Warnock herself has come to question the rationality of the Committee's recommendations (1991; 1992; 1997). Some of her regrets concern the 'horror of the present situation' (1997: 13) in which confrontation arises over provision (Chapter 6), but she also claims never to have enthused over the idea of integration:

> I was never very keen on integration — I was probably the least keen of all the Warnock Committee. What I was interested in was children with special needs who were already in the mainstream. I was not particularly keen on importing pupils with special needs from special schools because I could see the difficulties the mainstream would have. As I think we said rather carefully, integration can mean so many different things. If it only means having a unit for deaf children attached to a school, that's no good, but I am all in favour of a huge campus with everything together, providing the environment is friendly. But if it means integration in the classroom, I don't think so — although it is very difficult to generalise. (Warnock, 1997: 12)

Some commentators have questioned claims that the Warnock watershed represented progress, noting little change in terms of justice and equality (Barton and Landeman, 1993), although others, in criticizing the behavioural objectives approach within the Warnock report (Swann, 1983; Wood and Shears, 1986), imply that it was retrogressive, offering 'more opportunities for a process of segregation than for the reverse' (Swann, 1983: 121). Corbett suggests that the voice of enlightened modernity with which we celebrate progress is a voice of 'power, status and a confident authority' (1996: 15), which restricts thinking and justifies the continuation of patronage.

Attempts to give the pupils a voice have sought to provide an authentic reading of what it is like to have special needs. Cheston (1994), for example, explored pupils' explanations for being in special education, and Cooper (1993) asked pupils about their experience of being labelled as disaffected. Others have measured the self-esteem of individuals with special needs (Gibbons, 1985; Harvey and Greenway, 1984; Resnick and Hutton, 1987) or investigated their ability to cope in a mainstream school (Lynas, 1986b; Sheldon, 1991). Research on mainstream pupils (see Hegarty and Pocklington, 1981; Kyle and Davies, 1991; Lynas, 1986a) has produced superficial accounts of attitude towards, or acceptance of, pupils with special needs as some kind of generalized other, while ignoring what pupils say and do to each other. These essentialist perspectives construct pupils with special needs as objects upon which integration or inclusion is to be exercised.

The drive for representational clarity in educational research has ensured that the quest to rescue the researched from epistemic violence always fails (Lather, 1996; Stronach and Maclure, 1997). For pupils with special needs, this violence amounts to entrenching them as passive objects of research and 'excommunicating' them (Fulcher, 1995: 6) through a process in which 'researchers have benefitted by taking the experience of disability, rendering a faithful account of it and then moving on to better things while the disabled subjects remain in exactly the same social situation they did before the research began' (Oliver, 1992a: 109).

Stronach and Maclure's version of educational research as a 'strategic act of interruption of the methodological will to certainty and clarity of vision' (1997: 4) appears to be a much more relevant project for special education. It requires, however, asking a different set of questions about how and why integration, and subsequently inclusion, came to be the incontrovertible goal for pupils with special needs. The purpose, in asking these questions, is not to conduct an 'ontological search for the determinant-in-the-last-instance' (Gordon, 1980: 243) but to describe the configurations of these discursive shifts, where it has been 'necessary and sufficient for people to use these words rather than those, a particular type of discourse rather than some other type, for people to be able to look at things from such and such an angle and not some other one' (Foucault, 1980a: 211). It is also important to examine how the discourses of the present construct the identities and experiences of pupils with special needs and how individuals have resisted and contested these. Many deaf and blind people, for example, have preferred not to be known as hearing and visually impaired, but have fought to retain an identity that emphasizes, rather than euphemizes, their disability.

From Integration to Inclusion

Much of the commentary on integration has implied that it is a good thing, with little or no opportunity to depart from the moral and social imperative of mainstreaming. 'Those teachers still daring to actually *withdraw* children from their mainstream classes for *remedial tuition* must have felt like accomplices to some form of educational apartheid' (Payne, 1991: 61, original emphasis).

Mittler suggests that 'the fervour of integration has taken on the language of a religious revival' (1985: 9). However, as Booth notes, Mittler's urge to adopt instead a 'commitment to better education' or 'good practice' (1988: 99) tends to divert attention from the social and political contexts of integration and its role in obscuring and perpetuating inequalities. *The integrated child* emerged as a new binarism, which Marks (1994) argues could have been avoided, and Barton and Corbett have criticized 'the sterility of a rigid dichotomy between the virtue of integration set against the evils of segregation' (1993: 17). The increasing dissatisfaction with integration as a construct led to calls for its abandonment (Hegarty, 1993), replacing it with a more meaningful term which takes account of pupils' participation in the academic and social life of a mainstream school (Booth, 1988; Oliver, 1992b) and which avoids the 'dangerous complacency' (Barton and Corbett, 1993: 17) into which the 'new educational orthodoxy' (Oliver, 1992b: 23) has lapsed.

Inclusive education has crept up and become the new orthodoxy. Several writers have analysed the shift from integration to inclusion comprehensively (Barton, 1997; Clark et al., 1997; Uditsky, 1993), but it is important to highlight the different way of speaking about pupils with special needs which inclusion signals. Booth (1996) makes it clear that inclusion involves two processes: increasing pupils' participation within the cultures and curricula of mainstream schools and decreasing exclusionary pressures. The latter process requires that schools alter their ethos and practices to ensure that all children are included as a right. It also implies that there is no binarist artefact, *the included child*, since everyone is included and, more importantly, no-one is excluded. 'Inclusive education is about responding to diversity; it is about listening to unfamiliar voices, being open, empowering all members and about celebrating "difference" in dignified ways. From this perspective, the goal is not to leave anyone out of school' (Barton, 1997: 233).

There is, of course, a danger that inclusion could simply become a name for past practices, or that such radical change is simply seen as a symptom or an effect of 'policy hysteria . . . creating a climate of confusion and contradiction for educational development' (Stronach and Morris, 1994: 5). Uditsky (1993) is optimistic that schools and teachers will undertake the necessary reform to make inclusion work, but others remain more cautious. Skrtic, for example, expresses his fears that 'rather than resolving the special education problems of the late twentieth century, the inclusion debate will reproduce them in the twenty-first century' (1995: 234). Slee argues that so far schools have failed to alter their culture and practices in order to increase pupil participation and remove exclusionary pressures, suggesting that 'inclusion, a euphemism for containment and assimilation, ignores the need for deconstruction and recognition across a range of boundaries' (1996: 111). Corbett notes the replication of the binarities of inclusion/exclusion and asks: 'can inclusionism, in its most extreme form, become a form of politically correct bullying?' (1997: 57). The boundaries between inclusion and exclusion, as she suggests, are messy and ill defined and she uses Stronach's (1996) metaphor of a weaving cloth to explore the ambivalences of the boundaries and the ways in which individuals are simultaneously included and excluded. Research on inclusion requires significant epistemological shifts in order to understand pupils' experiences as partial and fragmented and to challenge the foundationalist basis of special education knowledge.

Theorizing special education

The dominance of the medical model within research on special education has been criticized by many writers (Clark, Dyson and Millward, 1998; Skrtic, 1995). The social model, the replacement offered by disabled writers such as Finkelstein (1980) and Oliver (1990), has been widely acknowledged as 'the big idea' (Hasler, 1993) behind the disability movement and has been greeted as a mark of progress in theorizing disability. Barton, for example, argues that the social model challenges the 'dominant orthodoxy' (1993b: 237) of the medical model in which 'disability is viewed in terms of an individual's inability to function' (ibid.).

The proponents of the social model have been less sure about its success. Shakespeare and Watson argue that the social model simply has not caught on among academics and point to the 'hostility and ignorance with which the social model is greeted in the wider world' (1997: 299). Oliver has been critical of the licence which some academics have taken within the scope of the social model for 'intellectual masturbation' (1992b: 20), in which able-bodied academics debate the lives and experiences of disabled people. As Oliver reminds us, the social model has a political perspective, and although progress in this respect has been negligent, he urges patience: 'because it cannot explain everything, we should neither seek to expose inadequacies, which are more a product of the way we use it, nor abandon it before its usefulness has been fully exploited' (1996: 41). Oliver attributes part of the blame for this to the disability movement itself which has had too much internal dissent over the nuances of the social model. Some of this dissent concerns the place of the body within the model (Chapter 8), and while many writers have joined with Oliver in calling for solidarity (Finkelstein, 1996; Shakespeare and Watson, 1997), others have remained more sceptical about the desirability of achieving a unified social model (Casling, 1993; Hughes and Patterson, 1997; Morris, 1991).

Research Relations

Considerable criticism has been levelled at researchers whose work has proved 'alienating' to disabled people (Oliver, 1992a: 103) by making them, not participating subjects, but objects upon which research is practised (Rowan, 1981). Where they have been asked to speak, they have been constrained to do so within professional discourses which construct them as objects of knowledge (Armstrong et al., 1993; Cooper, 1993). Barton (1993b) notes the increasing anger among disabled people (Finkelstein, 1993b; Morris, 1991) at researchers' disabling practices. Finkelstein (cited in Oliver, 1992a) has suggested a principle of no participation in research without representation and others (see Branfield, 1998; Oliver, 1992b) have questioned whether the able-bodied should be researching disabled peoples' lives at all.

This question needs to be addressed seriously by researchers. On the one hand, able-bodied researchers may lack empathy and run the risk of 'colonizing' the subjugated experiences of disabled people (Appleby, 1994; Opie, 1992). On the other hand, they may be well placed to challenge oppression by exploiting the privileges which come from their social position (Clough and Barton, 1995). Oliver (1990; 1992a) argues that both the disability movement and non-disabled sociology have a part to play in eradicating the oppression associated with disability. Clough and Barton call for a more 'sensitive and self-conscious research practice' (1995: 143) whereas others have argued for radical changes to the social relations within which research takes place:

> Disability research should not be seen as a set of technical, objective procedures carried out by experts but part of the struggle by disabled people to challenge the oppression they currently experience in their daily lives. Hence the major issue on the research agenda for the 1990s should be; do researchers wish to join with disabled people and use their expertise and skills in their struggles against oppression or do they wish to continue to use these skills and expertise in ways in which disabled people find oppressive? (Oliver, 1992a: 102)

A new approach, according to Oliver, would be centred on principles of reciprocity, gain and empowerment. What is also required from researchers is scrutiny of the power and knowledge relations within which the identities and experiences of disabled people are constructed and a surveying of the 'closure and repetitiveness in our own thinking' (Roth, 1992: 695).

Reasons to Be Cheerful?

Assurances of progress in special education by complicit researchers and commentators, who also provide further legitimization for pathologizing individuals' deficits, is disturbing, even if it is symptomatic of a more widespread drive for innocent knowing (Lather, 1996). It also exemplifies what Foucault calls the 'blackmail' (1984b: 42) of the Enlightenment project by constituting 'a privileged domain for analysis' (ibid.). There are, however, some grounds for optimism, with the prospect of strategies which mobilize meaning heuristically rather than exhaustively (Stronach and Maclure, 1997). Recent critiques (see Clark et al., 1997; Skrtic, 1995; Slee, 1996) have been effective, not only in accounting for mainstream schools' failure to undertake the necessary reform to become inclusive, but in specifying the changes required. Researchers have also recognized the need to study both inclusion and exclusion (Ballard, 1999; Booth, 1996) and in recent texts devoted to theorizing special education, researchers have been encouraged to adopt theoretical perspectives which disrupt a sense of progress, avoid pathologizing individuals' needs and take better account of their experiences (Clark et al., 1998; Haug, 1998). A willingness to change the relations of research production to ensure greater involvement of disabled people as 'expert knowers' (Barnes and Mercer, 1997: 7) has been articulated by researchers who have also undertaken to scrutinize their own non-disabled baggage (Ballard, forthcoming; Clough and Barton, 1995; Stone, 1997). As Zarb points out, however, there is 'still a long way to go' before the 'transformative potential' (1997: 49) of disability research is realized.

Disabled researchers have provided some comprehensive reflections on the research process (Barnes and Mercer, 1997; Oliver, 1997). These spell out clearly the obligations to disabled people, to ensure that both researcher and researched become mutually engaged in change (Lather, 1986; Oliver, 1992a). The ethical project of inclusion, outlined in the final chapter, specifies the responsibilities of everyone involved in inclusion research and practice. Each person is required to be attentive to the 'power/knowledge arrangements existing under their noses . . . that thwart and pervert their *good intentions*' (Blacker, 1998: 362, original emphasis). At the very least, it can spare researchers 'the indignity of speaking for others' (Deleuze and Foucault, 1977: 209).

Chapter 2

Foucault's 'box of tools'

Foucault offers a new way of understanding the complex experiences of children with special needs in mainstream schools and this chapter explores his contribution in both substantive and methodological terms. The strengths and weaknesses of a Foucauldian approach are considered, and it is argued that each of Foucault's analytical phases, archaeology, genealogy and ethics are helpful in analysing special needs. Furthermore, Foucault offers a number of strategies within his 'box of tools' (Foucault, 1977a: 208) in order to undertake the analysis. One difficulty, however, is that Foucault never conducted any of the empirical work that he insisted was necessary. Thus, the application of Foucault's ideas to special needs has required some creativity and the inspiration of other theorists, most notably Derrida (1972; 1990) and Bhabha (1994). The development of the analysis and the emergence of themes has been made explicit, in the hope of encouraging other researchers to 'add Foucault and stir' (Shumway, 1989: 161).

Foucault and Special Needs: Domains of Knowledge and Types of Power

The work of Foucault has significance to the study of special education in two respects. First, his analyses of discipline and punishment, medicine and madness have relevance to the experiences of children with special needs. Foucault describes how the criminal, the patient and the madman are constructed through disciplinary techniques, for example the 'medical gaze' (1973b: 29). Children with special needs could be said to be constructed in similar ways. Second, his methodology or 'box of tools' (Foucault, 1977a: 208) makes it possible to analyse both the official discourses on special needs and those operating within schools and classrooms. Ligget argues that it is necessary to become conscious of the 'institutionalized practices in terms of which disability is constituted' (1988: 264) in order to broaden the scope for political action. She warns, however, that the complexity of a Foucauldian approach should not be underestimated, whereas Skrtic (1995) points out that an anti-foundationalist analysis of this kind creates both a crisis and a possibility for special education knowledge.

The Subject and Power

Foucault's main interest is in the ways in which individuals are constructed as social subjects, knowable through disciplines and discourses. The goal of Foucault's work has been 'to create a history of the different modes by which, in our culture, human beings are made subjects' (1982: 208). In *The Birth of the Clinic* (1973b) and *Madness and Civilisation* (1967), Foucault traces changes in the ways in which physical and mental illness and abnormality were spoken about. Foucault employs a distinctive methodology for these studies (which he called archaeology), which aims to provide a 'history of statements that claim the status of truth' (Davidson, 1986: 221). In *Discipline and Punish*, Foucault analyses the techniques of power that operate within an institution and which simultaneously create 'a whole domain of knowledge and a whole type of power' (1977b: 185). This work is characterized as genealogy and sets out to examine the 'political regime of the production of truth' (Davidson, 1986: 224). Both archaeology and genealogy are concerned with the limits and conditions of discourses but the latter takes into account political and economic concerns (Shumway, 1989).

Foucault draws parallels between the disciplinary mechanisms within modern prisons and educational practices. Contemporary approaches to discipline and punishment and education may be regarded as more humanitarian than the systems of the past, but Foucault argues the reverse. The effects of the mechanisms of power, he contends, are to construct individuals as subjects in two senses: as subject to someone else, through control and restraint, and as subjects tied to their own identity by their conscience and self-knowledge. 'Both meanings suggest a form of power which subjugates and makes subject to' (1982: 212).

Surveillance

A central theme of Foucault's work is the way in which the 'gaze' constructs individuals as both subjects and objects of knowledge and power. In *The Birth of the Clinic*, Foucault illustrates how the medical gaze opened 'a domain of clear visibility' for doctors, by allowing them to construct an account of what was going on inside a patient and to connect signs and symptoms with particular diseases (1973b: 105). The space in which the gaze operated moved from the patient's home to the hospital and this became the site for the teaching as well as the acquisition of medical knowledge, the object of which was the body of the ill patient. The body of the madman, according to Foucault, was viewed as 'the visible and solid presence of his disease' (1973b: 159). Hence the medical gaze focused on the body and 'normalization' or treatment of the insane involved 'consolidation', 'purification', 'immersion' or 'regulation of movement' (Foucault, 1967: 159–72).

In his genealogical analyses of discipline and punishment and of sexuality, Foucault describes how 'the rather shameful art of surveillance' (1977b: 172), which occurs in relations between individuals (for example between children and adults), has an individualizing effect:

> In a disciplinary regime . . . individualization is *descending*: as power becomes more anonymous and more functional, those on whom it is exercised tend to be more strongly individualized . . . In a system of discipline, the child is more

> individualized than the adult, the patient more than the healthy man . . . when one wishes to individualize the healthy, normal and law-abiding adult, it is always by asking him how much of the child he has in him. (1977b: 193, original emphasis)

Foucault identifies three mechanisms of surveillance:

- hierarchical observation;
- normalizing judgments;
- the examination.

These techniques appear to shape many of the experiences of children with special needs and are so sophisticated that 'inspection functions ceaselessly. The gaze is alert everywhere' (1977b: 195).

Hierarchical Observation

The perfect disciplinary apparatus, according to Foucault, 'would make it possible for a single gaze to see everything perfectly' (1977b: 173). Foucault describes how the technique of 'panopticism' (1977b: 195), based on the design of Jeremy Bentham, was first integrated into the teaching relationship in the eighteenth century so that pupils could be observed at all times. It then became possible to combine hierarchical observation, teaching and the acquisition of knowledge within a single mechanism. 'A relation of surveillance, defined and regulated, is inscribed at the heart of the practice of teaching, not as an additional or adjacent part, but as a mechanism that is inherent to it and which increases its efficiency' (1977b: 176). Foucault views this mechanism as both efficient, since surveillance was everywhere and constant, and effective, because it was 'discreet', functioning 'permanently and largely in silence' (1977b: 177). It also supervised those who were entrusted with the surveillance of others.

Provision for children with special needs in mainstream schools has elements of this kind of surveillance. Children placed in a mainstream classroom are usually under constant and close observation. This supervision is hierarchical in the sense that many pupils are accompanied in mainstream classrooms by special needs auxiliaries or teachers; learning support specialists devise and oversee their programme of work and monitor how the mainstream teachers are coping; headteachers also require to be kept informed of the progress of recorded pupils in order to communicate this at formal review meetings to educational psychologists, parents and others. The surveillance does not stop at this point, as a network of reciprocal power relations has been created. 'This network *holds* the whole together and traverses it in its entirety with effects of power that derive from one another: supervisors, perpetually supervised' (Foucault, 1977b: 176–7, original emphasis).

All children are the objects of scrutiny within schools, but for pupils with special needs, the gaze reaches further. They are observed, not only at work in the classroom, but also during break times. The way in which they interact with mainstream peers or integrate socially is often viewed as equally important, if not more so, than their attainment of mainstream curricular goals. All aspects of the child's interpersonal relations can, therefore, be brought under the vigilance of staff. The emotional well-being of a child with special needs is also cited as an important aspect of special education. This legitimizes the search *within* the child for signs, for example, that he or she is happy or gaining confidence, to an extent that teachers would not scrutinize mainstream pupils. Surveillance of pupils with special needs enables professionals to show concern for their welfare and acquire knowledge about their condition and the progress they are making. It also constructs them as objects of power and knowledge:

> This form of power applies itself to immediate everyday life which categorises the individual, marks him by his own individuality, attaches him to his own identity, imposes a law of truth on him which he must recognise and which others have to recognise in him. It is a form of power which makes individuals subjects. (Foucault, 1982: 212)

Normalizing Judgments

Foucault observes how the Norm entered education and other disciplines, 'imposing new delimitations on them' (1977b: 184). It allowed institutions to establish 'The Normal' as a 'principle of coercion in teaching and as an instrument of surveillance' (1977b: 184). While this standardized education and promoted homogeneity, it also had an individualizing effect, 'by making it possible to measure gaps, to determine levels, to fix specialities and to render the differences useful by fitting them one to another' (1977b: 184). Normalizing judgments could thus be used to highlight difference and to seek to eradicate it through assimilating practices.

Children with special needs are defined in relation to normality by their very label. 'Special educational needs . . . as a rule of thumb . . . can be taken to include all children and young persons whose educational needs cannot be met by the classroom teacher without some help' (SOEID, 1996: 7). Those with the most significant needs are given a distinctive status through a statement or a Record of Needs. Yet the arbitrary cut-off point of 2 per cent of the population deemed to require such distinction has become a source of contention. Furthermore, it has come to signal additional resources and has become sought after by parents and others who willingly subject their children to the assessment process. They have come to recognize that the normalizing gaze of professionals can also be an auspicious one (Chapter 6).

The Examination

This technique, according to Foucault, combines hierarchical observation and normalizing judgment and 'establishes over individuals a visibility through which one differentiates them and judges them' (Foucault, 1977b: 184). In education it has taken a less ritualized form than, for example, in medicine, where the medical gaze allows doctors to construct an account of what goes on inside a patient, connecting signs and symptoms with disease. Three features of the examination enable it to function as a disciplinary technique:

- It imposes a principle of compulsory visibility, holding subjects in a 'mechanism of objectification' (1977b: 187).
- Individuality is introduced into the field of documentation. This makes it possible to classify individuals, form categories, determine averages and fix norms.
- Each individual is established as *a case* and may be 'described, judged, measured, compared with others, in his very individuality; and . . . trained or corrected, classified, normalized, excluded, etc.' (1977b: 191).

Foucault suggests that the examination is a technique which makes an individual an object of power and knowledge.

The assessment procedures leading to the opening of a Record of Needs or statement is a form of examination that 'leaves behind it a whole meticulous archive constituted in terms of bodies and days. The examination that places individuals in a field of surveillance also situates them in a network of writing' (1977b: 189). Before a multi-disciplinary assessment of a child with special needs takes place, the suspicion of abnormality needs to be voiced. This may occur at birth, when doctors observe genetic defects or trauma, or later on, when parents or teachers become concerned. The nursery or school provides a space where parents and teachers can compare a child against norms and any gaps provide evidence of abnormality. By the time the child undergoes a formal assessment, there is usually little doubt as to the existence of an abnormality or special need, although this notion of difference is, of course, socially constructed. The multi-disciplinary assessment, conducted from a variety of perspectives (for example, medical, educational and psychological), attempts to gain as much information as possible about the child and his or her home background, but is primarily a political and social process (Galloway, Armstrong and Tomlinson, 1994). This form of examination:

> clearly indicates the appearance of a new modality of power in which each individual receives as his status his own individuality, and in which he is linked by his status to the features, the measurements, the gaps, the 'marks' that characterize him and make him a *case*. (Foucault, 1977b: 192, original emphasis)

Following the assessment, the child with special needs is marked out for perpetual surveillance throughout the remainder of his or her school career and beyond. Parents and professionals also come under scrutiny as part of the continuous review of the recorded child's needs. All are caught by a gaze which is always alert to the deviant (Foucault, 1976); evidence of this provides a further rationale for surveillance of the general population (Ryan, 1991).

Spatialization

A final aspect of Foucault's analysis which appears relevant to the experiences of children with special needs is spatialization. Foucault shows how the practice of medicine, which began as a classificatory discipline, underwent two metamorphoses, becoming a medicine of symptoms before emerging as the clinical medicine which exists today. These were characterized by changes in the spatialization of disease and of medical treatment. The medical gaze altered the perceived space in which illness has its origin and distribution and the clinic 'was probably the first attempt to order a science on the exercise and decisions of the gaze' (1973b: 89). The treatment of madness also underwent radical change with the birth of the asylum as a punitive space. Foucault describes the asylum as:

> not a free realm of observation, diagnosis, and therapeutics; it is a juridical space where one is accused, judged, and condemned, and from which one is never released except by the version of this trial in psychological depth — that is, by remorse. Madness will be punished in the asylum, even if it is innocent outside of it. (Foucault, 1967: 269)

The superposition of the child and his or her special educational need is 'no more than a historical, temporary datum' (Foucault, 1973b: 3), yet its validity tends not to be questioned. The space in which special education is provided is also significant in relation to claims that a child is integrated. Ideal notions of integration are largely concerned with children with special needs and ordinary children sharing spaces, with the most pervasive sharing perceived as the most successful. Locational, social and curricular integration are regarded as progressive stages for pupils with special needs, but it is the increased physical proximity that is subjected to maximum surveillance and cited as evidence of integration. Increasing dissatisfaction with the spatial and technical connotations of integration have led to its replacement with the concept of inclusion (Chapter 1).

Archaeology, Genealogy, Ethics and Foucault's Analytical 'Tools'

Archaeology, which characterized much of Foucault's earlier work (1967; 1972; 1973a and b), facilitates a 'descriptive' account of discourses, essentially a history of statements that stood for the truth (Davidson, 1986). In special education, we should not be asking *why* we have become integrationist, and subsequently inclusionist, but *how* did integration and inclusion, rather than something else, come to be the dominant discourse within special education? This requires illumination of the discontinuities and oppositions within special education discourses, for example, from groups representing the deaf community or individuals with specific learning difficulties.

Foucault's later genealogical pursuits (1976; 1977b) focus on power/knowledge relations within institutions and reflect a shift of Foucault's interests from discourses to discursive practices and from a macro- to a micro-level of analysis. He urges others to analyse the 'micro-physics of power' (1977b: 29) by searching for 'points of resistance' (1976: 95). For pupils with special needs, this involves looking for evidence of them challenging the identities they are given or opting for alternative experiences. Foucault appears pessimistic about the possibilities of resistance, viewing technologies of power as so effective that individuals become willing agents in their own discipline. He argues that because power is positive, rather than negative, producing 'reality . . . domains of objects and rituals of truth' (1977b: 194), opportunities for resistance are closed off to individuals. This view was to change, however, with Foucault's final shift to ethics.

The study of ethics (1987a and b; 1988a and b) signals Foucault's turn towards the self and a much more sanguine view of human agency. Foucault envisions new possibilities of individuals challenging limits, fortified by his own practical experiences in the San Francisco gay community, in which 'he was practising an art of the self that was also a work on limits, living his philosophy as life' (Simons, 1995: 11). His notions of technologies of the self and transgression were not about finite transcendence of limits, but of ways in which individuals acquired new forms of subjectivity. This holds exciting prospects for pupils with special needs who no longer need to be viewed as passively constructed subjects, but as active agents who can challenge the limits imposed upon them and pursue alternative identities and experiences.

The main tool or strategy which Foucault uses within archaeology and genealogy is one of *reversal*. This entails examining official discourses which point to a particular conclusion, usually positive, and considering the implications of an opposite outcome (Shumway, 1989). In Foucault's studies of sexuality and madness he employs reversal to striking effect, showing, for example, that sexuality is not repressed and silenced, but is part of a whole proliferation of discourses. *Discontinuity*, another of Foucault's devices, encourages the search within historical discourses for gaps and disjunctures where change occurs. This requires abandonment of conventional notions of history as continuous and progressive and seems significant for special needs, given the certainty with which the 'Warnock report' has come to signify enlightened progress. Finally, *specificity* and *exteriority* require us to understand individuals and phenomena rather differently. Foucault cautions against regarding phenomena such as special needs as outside the discourses about them. Rather, the discourses which construct each phenomenon should be examined in the context of the particular period in which they were uttered. The discourses should also be viewed at their exterior, as unmotivated and unintentional, rather than having an internal rationality or irrationality. These strategies were useful for examining the ways in which formal and informal discourses included or excluded children with special needs from mainstream.

The most important strategy in this research was an unsettling of categories and an embrace of liminality which came, not from Foucault, but from Derrida (1972; 1990) and the anthropologist Bhabha (1994). Their work did not replace the Foucauldian perspective, but opened up new avenues in his work. Derrida's construct of 'undecidability', described as the 'violent difficulty of the transference of

a nonphilospheme into a philosopheme' (1972: 72), helped to explore the ambiguities and contradictions in the mainstream pupils' accounts of the identities and
experiences of pupils with special needs and their oscillation between medical,
charity and rights discourses. It was impossible for the mainstream pupils to define
these unambiguously because the process of naming 'enters the dialectic from both
sides at once (remedy–poison, good–bad, positive–negative and threatens the philosophical process from within' (Kamuf, 1991: 113). Bhabha's (1994) analysis of
post-colonialism highlighted the relevance of a Foucauldian theme of governmentality, 'the contact between the technologies of domination of others and those
of the self' (Foucault, 1988a: 19) to the mainstream pupils' accounts. It suggested
that they had an important role as inclusion gatekeepers, in which they both regulated and disrupted the experiences of pupils with special needs through their own
rules of conduct.

Boyne has already observed the 'mutual complementarity' (1990: 166) of
Derrida and Foucault and the lesson drawn from the debate between them that
'there is no pure other, that ontological difference is a chimera' (1990: 170). This
is, of course, an important message for pupils with special needs and for those who
seek to fix difference within them. Foucault's notion of transgression (1977c) was
important in examining resistance by pupils with special needs and their ways of
acquiring new forms of subjectivity and Bhabha's (1994) notion of hybridity in
relation to post-colonialism helped to explore this further. Bhabha suggests that a
refusal to have difference fixed by others interrupts the voyeuristic pleasure of the
identifier:

> That disturbance of your voycuristic look enacts the complexity and contradictions
> of your desire to see, to fix cultural difference in a containable, *visible* object. The
> desire for the Other is doubled by the desire in language, which *splits the differ-
> ence* between Self and Other so that both positions are partial; neither is sufficient
> unto itself . . . the very question of identification only emerges *in-between* dis-
> avowal and designation. It is performed in the agonistic struggle between the epi-
> stemological, visual demand for a knowledge of the Other, and its representation in
> the act of articulation and enunciation. (Bhabha, 1994: 50, original emphasis)

Bhabha's analysis suggested that resistance was agonistic, rather than antagonistic, involving a kind of playful struggle which Simons (1995) has likened to a
wrestling match. This seemed to connect with how the pupils spoke of trying to
contest some of the identities and experiences they had been given, not by a blatant
refusal, but through subtle strategies in which they nevertheless challenged their
oppressors, in this case their peers, teachers and others. Foucault's framework of
ethics was extended to examine the work which pupils, teachers, schools and researchers might do to further the project of inclusion (Chapter 9).

Foucauldian Research as Subversion

In order to bring Foucault into research on special needs, it was necessary to enter
the world of subversion and manipulation. The professional discourses within special

education had to be both scrutinized and undermined in order to allow children with special needs and their peers to talk. The pupils were assured that there were no right or wrong answers and that their side of the story was the only valid one, inciting them to speak by inferring a kind of counter-hegemonic power. The assumption of professional expertise in education had to be undermined to encourage the pupils to talk. The pupils needed to see the researcher as someone to be trusted and not in collusion with their teachers. It was important, therefore, to avoid being seen by the pupils as another teacher figure and to remain on the fringe of professional activities, however insecure for all. It was, of course, vital not to be so marginal as to be distant from the professionals and risk silencing their voices, but spending intervals in the playground, or laughing at pupils' deviant behaviour proved to be useful strategies. Statements which claim the status of truth about special education were examined in relation to particular vested interests. Policies were viewed, not as statements of intent, but as instruments of power/knowledge relations through which the identities and experiences of children with special needs are constructed. The Warnock and HMI reports were examined in relation to the official claims made. These were then tracked backwards until a dissenting or merely different voice was heard. Although analyses of the formal discourses are vital in understanding how identities and experiences are constructed (Allan, 1995), the emphasis in this book is on the informal discourses among pupils and teachers in schools.

Working in this subversive way was deeply disconcerting and there were many occasions when the security of professional discourses was tempting. Foucault's chronicle of a similar 'malaise' was reassuring:

> There was no clear status for psychologists in a mental hospital. So as a student in psychology I had a very strange status there . . . I was actually in a position between the staff and the patients, and it wasn't my merit, it wasn't because I had a special merit, it wasn't because I had a special attitude, it was the consequence of this ambiguity in my status which forced me to maintain a distance from the staff. I am sure it was not my personal merit, because I felt all that at the time as a kind of malaise. It was only a few years later, when I started writing a book on the history of psychiatry, that this malaise, this personal experience, took the form of an historical criticism or a structural analysis. (1988c: 6)

Foucault attributed his uneasiness to the ambiguity of his own status while working in a mental hospital and eventually began to see his peripheral role as privileged, from which he could observe without the demands of being part of the network. The subversive position within the schools gradually became less uncomfortable, helped also by those masters of deception portrayed in spy novels:

> Yet, as ever, nothing is one thing for long with Pym, and soon a strange calm begins to replace his secret missions. The silent, unlit country that at first sight appeared so threatening to him becomes a secret womb where he can hide himself,

rather than a place of dread. He has only to cross the border for the walls of his English prisons to fall away . . . 'I am a champion of the middle ground', he tells himself. (le Carré, 1986: 542)

Although Foucault's analysis and method appear to have considerable relevance to special education, there are obvious difficulties with imported theories of this kind. Foucault has attracted extensive criticism and it is important to be aware of the limitations as well as the possibilities of his theoretical framework.

Problems with Foucault

Habermas (1986) and Rorty (1990) see the problem with Foucault as lying in the tension between '. . . the almost serene scientific reserve of the scholar striving for objectivity on the one hand, and, on the other, the political vitality of the vulnerable, subjectively excitable, morally sensitive intellectual' (Habermas, 1986: 103). Rorty thinks it should be possible to do both, by making a more effective distinction between them, and labels Foucault the 'knight of autonomy' (1990: 2). Habermas, on the other hand, sees Foucault as ultimately unable to make value judgments and denounces him as a pessimist. His treatment of history and his failure to undertake empirical analysis has also received criticism. Some of these appear misplaced, whereas others are more convincing. The charge of pessimism, it would seem, arises from a failure to appreciate the possibilities within the final ethical phase of his work.

Fast and Loose Historian?

Foucault's approach to history is to isolate central components of social institutions and trace them back in time. In so doing, he shakes the cosiness that historians have traditionally enjoyed in the relationship of the past to the present (Poster, 1984: 74). As Shumway points out, he does not deal with a discipline directly, but rather describes its archaeology, 'which in this instance means the layers of sediment upon which it is built' (1989: 159). Foucault (1980b) claims only to have written 'fictions', which nevertheless induce 'effects of truth' (1980b: 193). He has been accused of playing fast and loose with historical data and time, selecting arbitrarily from sources (Marshall, 1989; Megill, 1979). Poster remarks that it is little wonder that he has been criticized by historians, since 'the evidential basis of the texts is odd and incomplete' (1984: 7). Megill, however, also argues that to accuse Foucault of inaccuracy is to miss the point of his work (1985) and suggests that Foucault should be treated as an animator, rather than as an authority.

Foucault eschews the notion of searching for origins and seeks instead 'to cultivate the details and accidents that accompany every beginning; it will be scrupulously attentive to their petty malice; it will await their emergence, once unmasked as the face of the other' (1984c: 80). By beginning with a diagnosis of the present situation, Foucault then makes it possible to ask 'How did we get here?' This requires attention to minute deviations within discourses which does not sit easily with charges of inaccuracy or selectivity.

Pessimism

> You would never guess, from Foucault's account of the changes in European social institutions during the last three hundred years, that during that period suffering had decreased considerably, nor that people's chances of choosing their own styles of life increased considerably. (Rorty, 1990: 3)

Perhaps the most serious criticism of Foucault's work is that he offers no recipes for social change. Foucault advocates local and continuous action to effect small changes but as Shumway points out, 'his work does little to encourage or instruct anyone interested in undertaking such action' (1989: 158). In addition, he insists that power necessarily entails resistance but 'gives the impression that resistance is generally contained by power and poses no threat' (Fairclough, 1992: 57). This criticism is particularly important for educationists, who may feel that there is little to gain from pursuing an analysis that denies, or at least fails to acknowledge, the possibility of action. It has been argued that it was Foucault's intention merely to 'diagnose the contemporary danger' (Dreyfus and Rabinow, 1986: 118) and that it is for us to resolve the conflict between his analyses and social change (Said, 1986). Fairclough sees the problem as arising from Foucault's tendency to reduce practices to structures and the absence in his work of 'real instances of people doing or saying or writing things' (1992: 57).

It may be that Foucault has been misunderstood and that he does indeed offer hope, *especially* for educationists, through the development of 'a critical ontology of ourselves':

> [This] has to be considered not, certainly, as a theory, a doctrine, nor even as a permanent body of knowledge that is accumulating; it has to be conceived as an attitude, an ethos, a philosophical life in which the critique of what we are is at one and the same time the historical analysis of the limits that are imposed on us and an experiment with the possibility of going beyond them. (1984b: 50)

This sounds far from pessimistic and seems to offer educationists the prospect of rethinking and evaluating educational practices. If education is approached with the 'limit-attitude', characterized by 'dissimilarity, constant decentring, endless deferral and recurring doubt' (Kiziltan, Bain and Canizares, 1990), it could '. . . translate into endless reconstructions, bringing about transformations in various aspects of public education, ranging from curricular to organizational restructuring' (Kiziltan et al., 1990: 366).

Rorty (1990) and Roth (1992) share the belief in the capacity of Foucault to transform education, providing, as educationists, we 'overcome our prefabricated self and fashion a new one courageous enough to dwell, nay thrive, in uncertainty' (Roth, 1992: 693). As Kiziltan et al. comment:

> In the labyrinth-like environment of the limit-attitude, life is guided not according to the promise of light or universal sociability but by a commitment to the overcoming and thus constitution of ourselves as autonomous subjects, an inherently collective project which always remains a beginning with each step we take, and each rearrangement of the maze that we coinhabit together. (1990: 369)

Disabled people face a double bind, since as Ligget (1988) points out, the price of speaking out about themselves is the acceptance of the disabled/non-disabled distinction within the normalizing society. This could well perpetuate, rather than challenge, disciplinary practices, but it is a risk which arguably is worth taking. Research has an important role in trying to find out how individuals become constructed subjects and in exploring ways in which they challenge their subjection, but requires more self-conscious and self-critical practice from researchers. There is scope for everyone associated with inclusion to treat it as an ethical project in which they do work on themselves as part of their responsibilities to others. Chapter 9 sets out the kind of ethical work which pupils with special needs, their mainstream peers, teachers, schools and researchers might practise in order to create more inclusive spaces.

Empirical Analysis

This final criticism relates to Foucault's failure to undertake any empirical work within institutions, despite contesting that this is the key to uncovering power/knowledge relations. Foucault claims that it is vital that social institutions are studied from an internal standpoint since they 'constitute a privileged point of observation, diversified, concentrated, put in order, and carried through to the highest point of their efficacity' (Foucault, 1982: 222). He is not, however, entirely convinced that institutions themselves are likely to yield conclusive evidence:

> One must analyse institutions from the standpoint of power relations, rather than vice versa, and that the fundamental point of anchorage of the relationships even if they are embodied and crystallized in an institution, is to be found outside the institution. (1982: 222)

Foucault has remained something of a global theorist, although as Fairclough points out, he claims to be talking about practice: 'his focus upon structures is intended to account for what can and does actually happen' (1992: 57). This does not mean, however, that empirical analyses of institutional practices cannot be accomplished and there are already some persuasive analyses of educational management (Ball, 1990b) and psychology (Walkerdine, 1984). Yet even these do not show how the disciplinary techniques work by providing examples of what is and is not said. This research examines the informal discourses of pupils and teachers and analyses the work they do on pupils with special needs.

Add Foucault and Stir?

Foucault's 'box of tools' helps to understand the identities and experiences of children with special needs in mainstream schools and make it possible to examine inclusion as a process, rather than as a single event. A Foucauldian analysis of discourses represents a departure from technicist–empiricist accounts of inclusion, which say more about where a child is educated or the forms of provision received than about the quality of their experiences. It focuses on the way texts and talk construct the identities and experiences of pupils with special needs and how they resist and contest this process and highlights the precarious nature of inclusion. As Skrtic (1995) suggests, research of this kind creates a crisis, since it 'calls the legitimacy of special education's knowledge, practices and discourses into question' (p. 37). It has an important role, therefore, in disturbing the complacency with which special education research and practice has conducted itself.

The pupils' voices dominate the remainder of this book, beginning with the mainstream pupils' accounts. Their interactions with pupils with special needs are arguably more important than resources or the kind of support provided, and Chapter 3 explores their involvement in the processes of inclusion and exclusion.

Chapter 3

Mainstream Pupils: Inclusion Gatekeepers

This chapter examines the role of mainstream pupils as inclusion gatekeepers, using their accounts and those of the pupils with special needs. It is argued that the mainstream pupils' accounts resist conventional binary divisions, for example, disabled/able-bodied; normal/deviant; or integrated/segregated, which fix the identity of pupils with special needs and place them either in or out of mainstream as a once-and-for-all event. Instead, identification and placement were continuous processes, liable to change at any moment within the ambivalences, contradictions and oscillations of the pupils' discourses.

The mainstream pupils' accounts oscillate around three interactive and competing discourses — medical, charity and rights. These discourses, which, according to Foucault (1976) both transmit and produce power, suggest how the pupils guide their own conduct and 'structure the possible field of action of others' (Foucault, 1982: 211). The mainstream pupils appeared to operate within a framework of governmentality (Foucault, 1988a; 1991a), functioning as a set of unwritten rules of conduct for themselves and others and sanctioning or prohibiting particular actions. Foucault's use of the term governmentality combines the power to direct conduct with a particular mentality or presumption that '*everything* can, should, must be managed, administered by authority' (Allen, 1998: 179, original emphasis). Foucault argues that it is a particularly insidious kind of government, since 'it incites, it induces, it seduces, it makes easier or more difficult; in the extreme it constrains or forbids absolutely' (1982: 220). It is made more complex by the imbrication of people and things, the way individuals are governed in their relationship with others and with objects such as 'resources . . . ways of acting and thinking . . . accidents and misfortunes' (Foucault, 1991a: 93). Bhabha (1994) describes the governmentality practised by colonizers as an avowed ambition to civilize or modernize. Among mainstream pupils, it could reflect a desire to normalize pupils with special needs or eradicate some of their differences.

Reading the Pupils' Regime

The mainstream pupils' governmental regime had a number of distinctive features. First of all, it involved the exercise of *pastoral power* upon the pupils with special needs, aiming for a kind of salvation (Foucault, 1982). This implied a protectiveness and concern for the well being of the pupils with special needs. It also gave the mainstream pupils a *pedagogic* role, in which they took responsibility for some of the academic and social experiences of the pupils with special needs. Occasionally their regime permitted *rule breaking* in relation to physical contact between pupils. Finally, it was *punitive*, legitimizing the exclusion of some pupils from social interaction. This regime of 'micro-governmental rationalities with prescriptive implications' (Simons, 1995: 37) enabled the pupils to distinguish between true and false statements (for example, concerning the best interests of the pupils with special needs) and develop rules and procedures and ways of achieving goals (for example, participation in mainstream or social interaction). Their regime operated just like any other political rationality, through discourses that 'make it seem as if techniques are addressing a common problem through shared logic and principles' (1995: 38).

Pastoral Power: 'They are humans'

The mainstream pupils expressed a great deal of concern for the well being of the pupils with special needs. In 12-year-old Phillip's case, this extended to concern for his physical safety, 'walking him home from school' and picking him up 'if he falls or that' because of his progressive physical disability. The mainstream pupils' pastoral power also oscillated between binarisms of deserving/undeserving and similarity/difference, which influenced their conduct towards pupils with special needs.

Deserving/undeserving

The peers of Brian, a 12-year-old with Down's Syndrome, talked about him with warmth, affection and frequent laughter because they 'loved being with him' and 'he was such a lot of fun', despite being 'a bit of a handful'. He had not been 'as lucky as them, when he was born', but 'they are humans, so should be treated the same as us'. 'They're really quite intelligent if you ask them the right things.' The mainstream pupils' pastoral power seemed to have a homogenizing effect upon Brian, reducing him to a generalized 'them'.

In contrast, Sarah (12) had been identified as having moderate learning difficulties, but some of her peers thought that she did not deserve the extra help she received:

C Some people think it's unfair that Sarah gets easier work.
A Quite a lot of the boys think that and think it's unfair that she gets a lot of help.
JA What do they say about that?
S They say, 'When we're stuck they don't help us.'
C But they just can't help everyone, although they do if you need it.
A They just resent her getting a bit more attention and they take it out on her.
JA Do they say anything to her about that?
C [Not] really, but they tell everybody else. If she's sitting in a different group, they'll just list her faults.

The peers of Scott, a 12-year-old with tuberous sclerosis, thought he did deserve help, unlike another child in their class with recorded special needs who appeared to have 'nothing wrong with her', but who was 'just too lazy and doesn't feel like doing the work'. One pupil said, 'I feel sorry for some of them, but not for [a girl with learning difficulties], because she smokes and drinks.' Scott also came out better than another child, a wheelchair user, who was thought to exploit his disability and therefore, did not deserve help: 'The week we were away . . . he was sitting there drinking his milk and he said, "watch this" and he chucked his milk carton away and made [his auxiliary] go and get it.'

The classmates of Peter, a 12-year-old identified as having emotional or behavioural difficulties, were highly uncertain about where to place him on the deserving/undeserving divide. This arose from their difficulty in understanding what was actually 'wrong with him'. Without the high visibility of a medical condition or some other clue to a disability, it was difficult for Peter's peers to make sense of his simultaneously odd and normal behaviour:

C   He's just a normal person, but has a disadvantage.
K   He's just a normal person, but in a different classroom [special unit], with one
    or two difficulties.

Peter's mainstream peers seemed uncertain whether or not he was able to control himself, hence their frequent qualifications in their statements, for example, 'He does show off a bit . . . but when he gets used to you, he'll work with you.' The pupils agreed that Peter's behaviour was his main problem, 'sometimes he goes wild', but they did not see him as completely uncontrollable: 'He stops it if the teacher gives him into trouble.' They seemed to see Peter as a boy who was capable of behaving, but who either chose not to or was unable to control himself from time to time. They had difficulty in distinguishing Peter's inability to do certain things from his apparent unwillingness:

In [Primary] 6 our project was tripods and we had to make a tripod and whenever I said, 'could you help me make it?', he would change the subject, so I had to make it all by myself. He's not lazy but when it's, like, using your hands or making stuff, he doesn't like doing it. I expect that's his worst subject, making things.

This account wavers in several directions. The mainstream pupil, finding Peter evasive, became somewhat resentful about having to 'make it all by myself', but then checked himself by saying 'he's not lazy'. He ended his diffidence on whether Peter avoided things he didn't like because of laziness or inability, by giving him the benefit of the doubt, saying, 'I expect that's his worst subject, making things.' This let Peter off to an extent, by implying an inability rather than a disability.

Speaking of the transfer to secondary school, the mainstream pupils harboured the usual worries about how they would fare themselves, but appeared more concerned about Peter's fate. 'When we're up in the Academy next year, I think the higher ones won't really know him and he'll get bullied.' Implied here is an intimacy with Peter and an understanding that despite his apparently normal appearances, he had significant problems. The pupils seemed to be protective towards him, fearing that strangers would respond to his 'odd' behaviour superficially (that is, fail to see it as a disability) and would be aggressive towards him.

Similarity/difference

The mainstream pupils articulated a binary divide of similarity and difference in terms of how individuals were 'like us/not like us', but were usually unable to place the pupils with special needs on either one side or the other. The following comments from the classmates of 11-year-old Susan, a wheelchair user, illustrate the mainstream pupils' uncertainty about how to treat her:

> G   I'd say treat her just like us.
>
> J   Yes, but try and help her as well.
>
> JA   Yeah?
>
> G   Help her as well, yeah, but just treat her like us, no offence or anything.
>
> JA   What do you mean by no offence?
>
> G   Well, I don't want to make her feel left out or anything. I think she should just join in whatever way she can. The same as we do.
>
> J   But try and help if she needs help, but try and treat her like us as well.
>
> G   Yeah.

The mainstream pupils seemed to be trying to erase difference as far as they could, by asserting that they should 'treat her like us'. Yet they acknowledged the importance of Susan being helped to feel better about her 'difference'. They also tended to attribute a homogeneity to individuals, as Brian and Scott's peers did when they spoke of a generalized 'them'. Phillip's peers commented: 'You don't try to make them feel that you don't want to talk to them. You just try and talk to everybody.' Some mainstream pupils offered evidence to support their claim that they were treating their disabled peers 'normally'. For example, one pupil, speaking of Barry, a 12-year-old wheelchair user, said that when she discovered a mistake she had made in a maths exercise she told, not only Barry, but other mainstream pupils about this to save them redoing it. This, she argued, showed that she was not 'treating him as a disabled person'.

For the peers of Raschida (17) and Laura (15), two visually impaired pupils, eradicating difference was an essential part of avoiding the taboo of seeing/not seeing: 'I'm OK now, it's just I wasn't really sure what to say. I was a wee bit nervous about saying things, like "Oh look at that, isn't that funny?" and her not being able to see it, I thought, "That's a bit nasty, I'll need to watch what I'm saying."' Their mainstream peers described how they sometimes found themselves in a state of uncertainty, wanting to help, but recognizing the dangers of signalling difference:

Sometimes I don't like to, I'd feel as if I'd patronize her by saying, "Here's a seat over here," but at the same time I'm trying to help her. I just don't know what to do sometimes . . . I'm afraid, afraid I'm doing that sometimes, but I don't mean to. I'm just trying to . . . go out my way to help her a wee bit.

According to Laura and Raschida, the discomfort of their mainstream peers was all too obvious and they found their attempts to avoid the seeing/not seeing taboo inept. 'They're frightened to mention about my eyes . . . in First Year they used to be dead wary in case they said anything.' Laura and Raschida had helped their peers to overcome some of their embarrassment; their strategies are discussed in Chapter 4.

The peers of Graham, a 16-year-old with moderate learning difficulties said they recognized and accepted his difference:

K   Sometimes he makes a bit of a fool of himself, but that's just . . . how he is, but you just ignore that and just get on with it. Apart from that, it's OK.

JA   What happens when he makes a bit of a fool out of himself?

K   It's just some of the things he says to the teacher. He calls Mr Wallace 'Sir'. He's just different from everyone else, but . . . we just leave him.

L   He's louder than everyone else all the time.

The mainstream pupils appeared to accept Graham as different and forgave his idiosyncrasies, since they caused no discomfort and offered some mild amusement. Yet these differences also appeared to legitimize some fairly punitive teasing to which they subjected him and which is discussed later in this chapter.

Pedagogic Strategies: 'He's getting a lot better'

The mainstream pupils seemed to see themselves as agents of the academic and social development of the pupils with special needs. Brian's peers, for example, described how they persevered with him for his own good:

But when you're asking him a question, sometimes he'll go 'don't know, don't know' when he does know. And you've got to keep asking him or he'll never know. You've just got to keep giving him attention and stuff at him, so that he'll know, because he knows all his colours and stuff and if you point to a colour he'll just say 'don't know that' or he'll say 'go away'.

The pupils said no one had told them 'how to behave', but felt that what they were doing 'would help him'. If he was being mischievous, they needed to be 'stern with him', otherwise 'he thinks it's a joke'. On one occasion he hid in a cupboard and the pupils cooperated with the teacher in disciplining him, despite finding the episode hilarious:

She walked past the cupboard and all she heard was this 'ah' and she looked in the cupboard and there was Brian sitting in the corner. They had given him into trouble and we were outside and he was sitting there crying [laughter]. It was dead funny, but . . . we weren't to laugh at him because he'd done wrong.

Brian's peers declared themselves satisfied with the improvements he had made, through being in their school and learning 'some of the same stuff' as them.

Peter's classmates also described their involvement in improving his behaviour and classwork:

> If he writes something down wrong, we'll tell him to do the right thing, or we'll tell him how to spell something. Unless we don't know how to spell it.

> I think he was just picked for us. We got Karen and Peter and the other half [of Primary 7] got Susan.

The comment that he was 'picked for us' set him out as both different from them and an object for them to practise their judgments about good behaviour and classwork upon. The pupils said they tried to involve him in class activities, but he sometimes 'spoilt things' by going over the top:

> C   Yesterday we put in a couple of his ideas.
> B   But if you tell him to give too much, he'll just really go overboard and say, 'You've got to chop people's heads off.'

The pupils' strategies for dealing with Peter's 'overboard' behaviour involved mainly ignoring him or laughing at him, to encourage him to stop 'telling you the same thing over and over again'. They said both were usually effective in making him stop. Yet, their accounts of these were tinged with an uncertainty over whether he really merited special treatment from them. This uncertainty seemed to be at its greatest when he behaved more like them (at their most disobedient). When he seemed to confirm his 'oddness', their governmentality acquired considerable leniency. They thought he had improved greatly since he had been with them, largely through their influence:

> B   He used to really talk.
> K   He's getting a lot better.
> JA What was he like before then?
> B   He would talk every time he saw you.
> J   Every time he saw anyone he knew, he'd just . . .
> P   When he tried to make a joke and it wasn't funny, you had to laugh or he'd keep on telling you the same thing over and over again.

Susan's peers praised her dependence on them for help, which they saw as a kind of boldness. 'She asks if she wants something. She'll just come out with it . . . If she wants something different she'll just ask. She's not scared to say anything. It just comes out.' They compared her to a more passive person, who would 'just sit there', without receiving their help. The peers of Sarah and Barry appeared less directly involved pedagogically. In Sarah's case, this might have stemmed from the view held by some that she did not merit extra help. They acknowledged, however, the impact on her self confidence of the bullying she experienced. Barry's peers simply seemed uninterested in him, either educationally or socially.

The mainstream pupils' experience in helping individuals with special needs led them to express more general views on inclusion. Brian's peers, for example, commented on the value to him and others with special needs from being in their class:

J   We like to be with them, help them what we can.

D   Help them to get better every day.

M   So that they will live up to, near enough, our standards, because near enough they need to go.

D   And also the feeling that you're actually doing something.

J   For other people.

D   Instead of just for your pleasure. Because they're getting a lot of pleasure out of it as well . . . Also, it's good experience for in later life, if there's someone in your job, if there's someone like Brian with Down's Syndrome comes and works with you, it's good experience because you kind of know what to expect.

Graham's peers also argued that his exposure to mainstream and to interaction with them was mutually beneficial:

K   Putting him into ordinary classrooms, like our English classrooms. I think if he went to other classrooms, I don't know if he goes into other classrooms, but if he does, being with other people. I'm not quite sure. And I think other people should be able to go into normal classrooms and get used to it. I think it helps us too to have more respect for them, because I used to think people from the special unit didn't actually have to do anything there, so I didn't have much respect.

L   They do seem quite immature when they're just in the unit . . . I knew Graham when he was just in the unit, but ever since he's come into our class, he really has matured quite quickly. Because he used to just muck around, make quite a fool of himself . . . He used to hit the girls and tell them to shut up, but he's changed quite a bit now.

The mainstream pupils' comments convey a sense of the special unit as a form of incarceration, albeit with a relaxed regime in which the pupils did not have to 'actually do anything'. They suggested that Graham had made improvements through his contact with them in mainstream classes, although he hadn't stopped 'making a fool of himself'. They said they had learned some 'respect for them', yet, this was tinged with surprise, as if they had expected Graham and others to founder in mainstream.

Susan's peers were less emphatic about inclusion, arguing that she benefited from being both in their class and in the special unit:

B   I think they should be in both, like in our classroom and in their own class.

JA   Why do you say that?

T   Well, it would be nice to know that some other people are in wheelchairs and everything and again it would be nice to know that you can be with other people that haven't got the problems.

JA   What do you think, Jane?

J   I think that it's good for her to be in our class sometimes and then to be in her class.

JA   So you think the same as Tony. Is that for the same reasons?

J   Yes. She's got lots of things here now and she's got her bars to help her.

Part of their justification for advocating both inclusion and exclusion for Susan came from their view that she should interact with others who shared her differences and who could empathize with her in ways that they could not. Thus, the pupils seemed to place her in a double bind of similarity and difference in which she belonged neither entirely with themselves nor with her 'own kind', but somewhere in between.

Breaking Rules: 'He's always kissing Denise'

The mainstream pupils' regime seemed to permit rules concerning intimacy between pupils to be breached. These rules normally prohibit physical contact and public displays of affection, at least within the school, but they did not apply to Brian. His peers described how they were unfazed by his penchant for kissing them:

> He's always kissing Denise, she's his favourite . . . The worst thing that Brian can do — he's just had his Milky Way, he's not had a drink and if you don't tell him to go and wipe his mouth he'll come over . . . and give you a kiss . . . You've got a white shirt or a blue one, he'll give you a kiss and it goes right over your shirt [laughter]. Especially if it's a Monday and you've just come in with a clean shirt. You've got to go home at three o'clock . . . and have a clean one for Tuesday.

Being kissed by Brian was seen as legitimate, yet the pupils made it clear that this was not acceptable behaviour towards anyone else. They said they had no qualms about crossing this normally well defined boundary with Brian, and their main concern was the Milky Way stain which usually followed such an exchange. However, even this was read by the pupils within an educational discourse, peppered with concern for 'good signs', in which they argued that his increasing ability to wash his own face signalled progress: 'You'll maybe need to remind him sometimes, but mainly he'll go and kind of try and do it himself. Which is another good sign, because . . . you know he's learning.'

Denise, the main object of his affection, laughed as she recalled, 'I got a big kiss and a cuddle from him at lunchtime today. I couldn't exactly refuse.' Denise, like Brian's other peers, found his affectionate behaviour both unstoppable and desirable, viewing it as typical of the exuberant and friendly way people with Down Syndrome behave. When it appeared more than that, for instance, involving close contact and touching with possible sexual overtones, Denise said she felt uncomfortable. Yet having sanctioned behaviour not usually open to other pupils it was difficult for her to redraw boundaries by pulling away from him:

> Sometimes, it's a little bit embarrassing because sometimes he does it in front of the whole class . . . when I was in the class last year with him, he did it in front of the whole class. [For example], if we were just about to go for gym or were sitting in the hall for assembly, he would sit and he'd rub my knee or he'd rub my hand. It was if he was trying to . . . I don't know, kind of get closer to me. Not as in a kind of friendship way, but something else.

Sexual taboos which operate under normal circumstances within school seemed capable of being breached within the de-sexing discourses of disability. Denise's uneasiness seemed to stem, not from the breach itself, but from how other mainstream pupils interpreted it.

Punitive Authority: 'He doesn't bother'

So far, the mainstream pupils' regime seems to have been largely positive and supportive, helping pupils with special needs to succeed. It was also, at times, highly punitive and legitimized the exclusion of individuals from social interaction, as the experiences of Graham and Scott suggest. Graham's mainstream peers said they talked to him occasionally, to 'humour him' and entertain themselves over his obsession with football:

L   They just tease him a bit.
M   Yeah.
K   It's all . . . good fun, really.
JA   What happens?
M   They'll say things, like, 'Did you go to see the Aberdeen match?'
K   Yeah, they'll tease him about another team playing against them and if they beat Aberdeen, they'll take the mickey out of him. It's all in good fun, really.
JA   How does he react?
M   He takes it as a joke.

Graham made no reference to such episodes, joking or otherwise. The mainstream pupils, however, said that he sometimes responded to teasing by saying that he was going to tell the teacher. That, to them, was going 'a bit far', since 'other people would just, like, take it' and so his response marked him out further as different from others. It also suggested an insulating divide between the mainstream pupils' governmentality towards Graham and more conventional pupil regimes, in which teasing was both given and received. Graham seemed to be disqualified from crossing this boundary by his inability to 'take it'. His objections to their teasing could be interpreted as resistance, but for the mainstream pupils, they seemed merely to affirm his difference. Beyond this, Graham was usually ignored when he drew attention to himself, for example, by being loud.

Scott said his other name was 'brain dead'; at least that was the one he had heard his classmates call him. They offered the additional names, 'Radar' and 'Alien', 'because of the shape of his head', which made him look as if 'he's come down from space'. The mainstream pupils described Scott's names amid much laughter. One boy, almost hysterical, said that 'everyone says that his forehead is like a radar', then added, 'I don't say that, I just find it funny.' They pointed out that people in the class had to be really different to earn a name like that, 'I mean look at Steven there with a flat face and no-one laughs at him.' The pupils seemed to see this naming as both sufficiently unacceptable to distance themselves from it, by suggesting that the perpetrators were other people, and legitimate, because 'everyone has a name in the class'. These other names, however, were usually self-selected. Their justification that Scott did not mind his names contained some uncertainty:

L   He doesn't bother.
S   He doesn't do anything.
C   He just laughs.
L   He sometimes laughs . . . or he tries to fight back.

In the hierarchical and normalizing playground, Scott was usually the last to be picked for games and although it might be considered a success for him to be included at all, the process was also excluding, by providing an opportunity for further ridicule:

We were playing a game the other day called speedball and he was last to get picked and they were going 'no we don't want him, [you] have him' . . . They weren't saying they didn't want him but they said 'Oh no it's your go, [you] take him' and all that.

This was not, they said, done blatantly, but in a way that was not likely to be 'picked up' by Scott:

T   Some of the boys say 'we don't want you in our team, you go in the other team' then the other team don't want him. So it ends up that you don't exactly say it but it's a you're not having him, they're not having him.
C   Or they'll say 'he's good' and they'll wink at each other. He's always last to get picked and everything.

He was not, they said, able to apprehend this treatment or the names they called him:

T   They just sort of say things that everybody laughs at but he doesn't really know that they're talking about him sometimes.
JA Can you give me an example?
C   Well, Tina called him a spazzy once to his face but she didn't call him it to his face, she called Neil it.

Scott's apparent inability to perceive these events had a licensing effect on the pupils, yet they acknowledged some resistance from him. 'Sometimes he sticks up for himself because sometimes he can be very cheeky back.' Scott's perceived lack of awareness seemed to extend the boundaries of acceptable conduct to include fairly vicious exposure of his playground incompetence. The mainstream pupils' judgments about Scott's perceptions tended not to be pedagogic, but related to permissible levels of teasing which were likely to be missed by him but not by the other pupils. Scott revealed the names his peers called him along with other pupils whose difference had also made them the focus of scorn. A small boy had been called 'smout'; another, with big ears, was renamed 'jug'; a third had been ridiculed in drawings and named 'moustache' after a single hair had appeared on his lip. Scott and his fellow victims said they felt 'heartbroken' to be treated this way and Scott added, 'I get really hurt when people call me brain dead . . . Nearly everyone is different, they've got talents and things they can't do.'

Policing Conduct

The operation of the mainstream pupils' governmentality involved on-the-spot judgments about how to act. It also involved policing their own conduct and that of their peers. Their policing enabled them to sanction certain kinds of behaviour and prohibit others, although this too was often surrounded by uncertainty. In some cases the pupils simply hovered in a state of indecision, for example, as Sarah's peers did when they saw she was upset. According to Foucault, policing is concerned, not merely with the criminal, but with 'the whole array of factors making up a healthy, productive population' (Ransom, 1997: 62).

Brian's peers criticized some of their classmates for being too sentimental towards him:

J   Well there [are] some people [who] overprotect them, overtreat them, instead of treating them equally.

D   They make it more obvious that they are actually special.

J   They hold hands with Brian and they don't need to do that.

D   They make everything really simple for them, but we can attempt to make it a wee bit more difficult, just for them to understand, so that they're learning every day, but they can still kind of basically communicate with us . . . And if there's no answer from either of them, then they'll just keep repeating it, whereas if we're saying it, we'll just say it the once, maybe twice, but after that we'll just leave it because we'll know that they have heard it.

They also took to task some pupils who called anyone who behaved stupidly 'Jim', pulling a face at the same time. They saw this as abusive because it referred to an older person outside school, who, like Brian, had Down's Syndrome. They seemed to be less concerned by Jim's reaction to this than by the inferred association with Brian:

If they say something about Jim it exactly means what they're meaning about Brian because Brian's just, he's not . . . the same as Jim but he's kinda a wee bit and we think that's not fair to do that to him when he hasn't done anything to them, so why should they do something to him?

Peter's peers indicated that some children in the school had called him names and in criticizing this, they reinforced his 'special' identity, arguing, for example, that it was 'unfair to keep on calling him names, just because he's got special needs'.

Graham's peers, despite subjecting him to intensive teasing over his obsession with football, had established limits to acceptable behaviour towards him, beyond which they would feel uncomfortable. 'If someone was doing something to him, like picking on him or something, we'd feel a bit of resentment towards them.' The pupils inferred a somewhat passive reaction in their imagined 'resentment' to any treatment of Graham which crossed their own boundaries of appropriate conduct, but such a situation had not arisen, so it was difficult for them to be more than speculative.

Scott's mainstream peers were critical of treatment he received from one of their classmates who had stepped over their boundaries of acceptable behaviour:

M David sometimes teases him if they're playing at football.
A If they're playing at football, he's not that good with his legs, because of his [condition] and he usually misses it and he'll start shouting at him.
M Today he came up to him and said 'I've got three times the energy of you — you can't even kick a ball. I'm in the football team, you're not.'

They said they had also stepped in to stop Scott being 'picked on' by the school bully:

Sometimes with Scott at football training a boy called Pat always slags him and . . . bullies him. [For example] he was playing against him that Monday and his team won and at the end he just came at him and threw him down on the ground . . . and me, Gary and Brian just told him to stop it.

Scott's peers legitimized their own excluding practices on the grounds that he was unaware of them, even though Scott indicated that he was, but prevented more overt maltreatment from taking place. Their governmentality, although subtle in its distinction between different kinds of conduct, appeared also to be imprecise in judging the effects of that conduct.

The mainstream pupils in Sarah's class expressed their indignation at the way she was treated, particularly by one individual:

S Some people give her a hard time. Like Sam says, 'What are you looking at me for?' and she's doing nothing of the sort. He just noises her up and glares at her.
A It's [not] fair because Sarah [doesn't] do anything.
JA Why do you think he does it?

C Just to annoy her.

S I think she got a bit upset about that a while ago.

C She cries a lot.

A He was starting to threaten her a lot and she got really upset about that.

C Sometimes if I've come in from lunch you see her crying and that you know that 'cos her eyes are all watery.

The pupils said Sarah was isolated in a variety of ways. In basketball, for example, no-one passed the ball to her 'because they think she's not good at other subjects'. She was also left out of the class repartee. Although they said Sarah 'usually keeps out of it', they were unsure how much of this was by choice:

A I don't think it really bothers her.

C But I think she sees other folk . . . enjoying themselves and she thinks she can't join in.

A I don't think it really bothers Sarah that much to be, you know, left out. I think if it were to happen all the time, it would bother her, but I think it [doesn't] really bother her.

C I think if everybody got along better with her she'd do better. She'd join in the stuff and that.

S I think if Sam got on better with her it would make her feel better about herself.

C She'd be more confident. Sometimes you think she's [scared] to come to school and it's because she knows that something's going to happen or someone's going to say something to her.

A But it is really Sam who does it.

Their blame appeared to focus on Sam, but they were reluctant to act on Sarah's behalf:

A Somebody needs to tell Sam that you can't treat people like that.

C But sometimes you can't tell the teacher about that because they'd just annoy you even more.

S I think she'd maybe not want us to say anything in case it started a big fuss over her.

The mainstream pupils rationalized their own inertia on the grounds that to do something would make things worse for Sarah and for them. They were caught in a double bind of trying to do what was best for Sarah, while maintaining their own status within the classroom. The 'somebody' who needed to stand up to Sam, therefore, became the teachers:

C They should teach us how to deal with it and that. Because people don't know about it and they just think it's up there.

A They should give us advice on how to treat them because people . . . say things. People wouldn't tease her as much.

These comments show both a collective responsibility for and a distancing from her ill treatment. The mainstream pupils also argued that they should all be taught about how to deal with 'them', so that 'people' wouldn't tease her as much. Without guidance of this kind, Sarah faced a bleak future:

C   If people keep annoying her she won't have much of a future.
A   She'll be too worried about what other people are saying about her.
S   And she'd be too scared to go for jobs and get married and that, in case people say no.

The pupils were calling for more support from teachers, who were, however, oblivious to the bullying Sarah had experienced and to her tearfulness in class.

At the Gate Alone?

The mainstream pupils' accounts suggest that they have a key role as inclusion gatekeepers. Their governmental regime, with its pastoral and pedagogic features, seemed mostly to support and guide the inclusion of pupils with special needs and enabled some of the conventional rules between pupils to be broken. But the regime also legitimized the exclusion of some pupils, for instance Scott and Sarah, by permitting certain actions by the mainstream pupils. The ambivalence within the mainstream pupils' accounts created at times a state of uncertainty, in which they were unsure what to say and how to act and which enforced a disabled identity for some pupils. It sanctioned both inclusion and exclusion, placing the pupils with special needs in neither one state nor the other, but in a state of 'undecidability' (Derrida, in Kamuf, 1991: 112) somewhere '*in-between* disavowal and designation' (Bhabha, 1994: 50, original emphasis). The way in which Graham's peers both enabled and prohibited his inclusion by discussing football, while also withholding some of the unwritten rules about this particular discourse, illustrates the subtlety of the process. A healthy obsession with football is part of being a young Scottish male, yet somehow Graham had misjudged the appropriate level of interest and had become an object of ridicule.

The mainstream pupils' governmentality, although broadly supportive of inclusion, was highly regulating and normalizing, and their perseverance, criticism, resentment and indignation acted as self-regulatory mechanisms, policing their own conduct and that of others. Like any other governmental regime, it constructed the subjects it governed (Allen, 1998) and its functionalist orientation to creating useful individuals (Gordon, 1991) imposed limits on pupils with special needs, by contributing to the construction of their disabled identities and constraining them to act in particular ways. The pupils with special needs, however, were not passive recipients of the mainstream pupils' governmental regime. Their attempts to resist and contest the mainstream pupils' regime and, in some cases to work directly on it, is explored in the following chapter. Foucault's interest in governmentality has ranged from the relationship of self-to-self and of self-to-others to the exercise of political sovereignty (Gordon, 1991) and has focused particularly on how the gradual imbrication of state and pastoral power has become increasingly individualizing (Brown, 1998; Foucault, 1988d). The mainstream pupils' governmental regime was concerned with 'the government of one's self and of others' (Gordon, 1991: 2) and has been analysed in terms of its rationality or 'system of thinking about the nature of the practice of government' (1991: 3). The purpose of doing so is to heighten awareness of the gatekeeping role of mainstream pupils and to try to make their regime 'thinkable and practicable both to its practitioners and to those upon whom it is practised' (1991: 3).

Chapter 4

Transgressive Practices: Shaping the Self

Introduction

The voices in this chapter are those of six pupils with special needs, who sought to challenge the identities and experiences which had been constructed for them within formal school regimes and the informal discourses of teachers and pupils. These efforts are described by Foucault as 'technologies of the self' (1988a: 11), acts of resistance, which 'are not something that the individual invents by himself. They are patterns that he finds in his culture and which are proposed, suggested, imposed on him by his culture, his society and his social group' (Foucault, 1987a: 122). Technologies of the self are transgressive and involve, not direct confrontation or antagonism, but a much more agonistic kind of struggle against those who attempt to label them as disabled or restrict their participation within mainstream class-rooms. These practices

> permit individuals to effect by their own means or with the help of others a certain
> number of operations on their own bodies and souls, thoughts, conduct, and a way
> of being, so as to transform themselves in order to attain a state of happiness,
> purity, wisdom, perfection or immortality. (1988a: 18)

The transformation Foucault refers to does not involve a transcendence, but a transgression from one kind of self to another.

The practices of Raschida, Laura and Barry involved transgressing out of disabled identities as visually impaired or physically disabled. Susan and Peter, in contrast, appeared to be transgressing *into* a disabled identity, as a dependent wheel-chair user or, in Peter's case, with a more visible disability than his emotional or behavioural difficulties suggested. Phillip, who was losing mobility through muscular dystrophy, practised a much more ambivalent kind of transgression in both directions. The pupils' transgressive actions, regardless of direction, were highly precarious and were practised with the constant threat of coercive markers of disability. Although for Raschida, Laura, Barry and, in most cases, Phillip, these coercive markers restricted their scope for transgression by forcing them to be disabled, they helped Susan and Peter and occasionally Phillip, to transgress. These coercive markers were laid down either by formal medical and charity discourses of disability, for example, physical items such as a white cane or guide dog, or informal discourses such as the mainstream pupils' sympathetic attitudes. The teachers'

discourse of needs, which required the pupils to accept help and public acknowledgment of their disability, also acted as a coercive marker of disability. The
mainstream pupils' governmental regime (Chapter 3) was occasionally punitive and
thus acted as a coercive threat. More usually, however, the mainstream pupils'
regime operated collusively to support the transgressive actions of Raschida, Laura
and the others. The precarious nature of transgression required pupils to engage in
a kind of policing of boundaries around their own selves. They also needed to work
on their mainstream peers' governmental regime to encourage them to catch the
ordinariness of their transgressive actions. As a result, transgression was never
accomplished entirely, but had to be constantly repeated, giving the pupils a kind of
liminality (Turner, 1969). Their new identities had the quality of 'undecidability'
(Derrida in Kamuf, 1991: 112), encountered by their mainstream peers, in which
they were neither disabled nor 'normal', but participated in the fusion of boundaries
(Haraway, 1991). The chapter begins by addressing the question of what counts
as transgression, before reporting the six pupils' accounts of this process. The
transgression of Fiona, a hearing-impaired pupil, is considered in a separate chapter
(Chapter 7) because of the complexity of deaf identity and culture.

What is Transgression?

As Foucault reminds us, the individual is a disciplined object formed by 'a policy
of coercions that act upon the body' (1977b: 138). This means that 'we are objects
of social institutions and processes while we intentionally engage in behaviour'
(Cherryholmes, 1988: 35). At the same time, however, Foucault urges us to break
out of the individualizing and totalizing power structures and to 'promote new
forms of subjectivity through the refusal of this kind of individuality which has
been imposed on us for several centuries' (1982: 216). Foucault's analysis of disciplinary mechanisms within institutions have been so convincing that it is difficult to
see possibilities for individuals breaking through the modes of subjection. Furthermore, Foucault fails to elaborate on how individuals might resist (Simons, 1995;
Taylor, 1984), even though he suggests that since the body is so often the target of
power, it should also be the instrument of resistance (Foucault, 1976). He also
argues elsewhere that the body 'is totally imprinted by history' (Foucault, 1984c:
83) and is therefore contaminated. The injunction to transgress seeks magically to
erase such contradictions and appears thus as a form of ontological rescue. Yet,
transgression appears to offer scope for a kind of creativity which does not promise
complete freedom, but enables alternative versions of constraint.

Foucault looked forward to the day when transgression 'will seem as decisive
for our culture, as much part of its soil, as the experience of contradiction was at
an earlier time for dialectical thought (1977c: 33). One of the difficulties in trying
to examine transgression concerns the absence of a language in which to describe it.
It is possible, however, to say what transgression does. Most importantly, transgression involves the challenging or crossing of limits or boundaries imposed by
others:

> Transgression, then, is not related to the limit as black to white, the prohibited to the lawful, the outside to the inside, or as the open area of a building to its enclosed spaces. Rather, their relationship takes the form of a spiral which no simple infraction can exhaust. (1977c: 35)

Foucault suggests that transgression has its entire space in the line it crosses and recrosses and is both simple, regulated by obstinacy, and complex, in its concern for upsetting already uncertain contexts. It is a continuous and playful act of 'agonism' (a more subtle kind of challenge than antagonism) which seeks to laugh in the face of those who have tried to impose limits. Transgression is an ambivalent act of non-positive affirmation which 'neither repudiates the place from whence it came nor welcomes the place to which it is bound' (Boyne, 1990: 82). Foucault likens transgression to Blanchôt's notion of 'contestation', which 'does not imply a generalized negation, but an affirmation that affirms nothing' (1977c: 36). According to Foucault, transgression does not transcend limits, since that would be to end being, nor transform individuals; rather, it provides an unstable space where limits are forced. Yet, the effort of going beyond limits can paradoxically reinforce them, since

> transgression contains nothing negative, but affirms limited being — affirms the limitlessness into which it leaps as it opens this zone to existence for the first time. But correspondingly, this affirmation contains nothing positive: no content can bind it, since, by definition, no limit can possibly restrict it. (1977c: 35–6)

In other words, transgression allows individuals to peer over the edge of their limits, but also confirms the impossibility of removing them.

For those who transgress, 'otherness lies ahead' (Boyne, 1990: 82) in new forms of subjectivity. It allows individuals to shape their own identities, by subverting the norms which compel them to repeatedly perform, for example, as gendered or disabled subjects (Butler, 1990). They need not reject their gendered or disabled identities, but can choose to vary the way in which they repeat their performances, cultivating an identity which is always *in process*. Shildrick and Price suggest that self-help groups for 'ME sufferers' (1996: 107) might be a form of collective transgression against 'regulatory norms' (ibid.) which have produced 'differing reinscriptions of the bodies of those with ME' (ibid.). Transgression, then, might be practised individually or by groups. Lloyd and Thacker (1997) warn against reifying transgression as a universal principle such that every transgressive act or practice is praised uncritically for its own sake and Foucault emphasizes the need to maintain the option to transgress or not. He urges caution in the pursuit of transgression, as it may not be possible or desirable for all, and argues that 'this work done at the limits of ourselves must . . . put itself to the test of reality . . . both to grasp the points where change is possible and desirable, and to determine the precise form this change should take place' (1984b: 46). Indeed, acts of transgression by individuals may conflict with the interests of others, as was the case with the six pupils in this chapter. It may be possible to help pupils to evaluate these conflicts and the limits of their transgression within a framework of 'critical ontology' (1984b: 50).

Transgressing out of Disability

Raschida and Laura

Attempts by Raschida and Laura to transgress their visually impaired identity involved working both on their own 'normal' appearances and on their peers' awareness of this. They rejected several coercive markers of disability, such as the long white cane, guide dog and rehabilitation training. In one instance, Laura provided her own by mistaking a flower vase for a vinegar bottle in a restaurant, but her repair was swift. Their mainstream peers were mainly collusive, supporting their attempts at being normal, but their uneasiness about visual impairment and concern about saying and doing the right thing also made them coercive markers of disability. The girls' efforts to make their peers less 'uptight' removed some of them and allowed their peers to be more supportive. The teachers, on the other hand, provided the most intransigent disability markers by forcing Raschida and Laura to accept their help (Chapter 5).

Both Raschida and Laura rejected the long white cane given to them to assist their mobility. Raschida giggled as she told how she managed to lose hers in a lake, by testing the depth of the water. She had subsequently been given a smaller one which could be folded up when not in use. The pupils refused to undergo mobility training with a rehabilitation officer anywhere at home or at school where they might be seen by friends. Controlling their peers' awareness of their impairment by appearing to be coping with everyday tasks was important to the girls and this would be spoiled if they were seen 'with a white stick or a dog' — 'I'd die on the spot,' said Laura.

Raschida and Laura had become so accomplished at making their way around the school that 'nobody really can tell, hardly' (Raschida). They indicated that pupils in their mainstream classes found their 'difference' difficult to deal with. One effect of this was that issues about seeing and not seeing became taboo in their presence and the girls were aware of the difficulty and embarrassment caused by trying to deny the existence of their impairment. As a result of this, Raschida and Laura had developed pedagogic strategies, aimed at educating their mainstream peers out of any discomfort over their impairment. This mainly involved self deprecating humour. 'Sometimes people are uptight . . . in the beginning everyone was uptight about your eyes, but you just make jokes about it all the time and just forget about it. Especially Raschida and me, we always seem to make a fool out of each other (Laura).

They said this had worked well, as 'everybody's so used to laughing now . . . they treat it as a joke'. Raschida also said that a 'slagging off' she had received from mainstream pupils for ignoring them in the street, even though they knew she could not see them, signalled a breakthrough in her relations with them. Laura cited an example of how her best friend had not only responded to her jokes, but had also begun to make some of her own:

> In first year, they used to be dead wary in case they said anything, but I remember
> a couple of weeks ago, Linsey was going on about OIS [Office and Information

> Skills]: she's always looking at the [computer] keys and she's always getting into trouble. I [said] to her, 'I never look at the keys, I just look at the screen' and she says, 'I know, you'd get caught.' She never used to be like that, she used to be dead wary, but she's used to me now, because I'm always saying something like that.

Things were much easier for them, they said, if people were not constantly 'uptight' or 'falling over themselves to help or say the right thing'.

The pupils' transgressive actions were not singular accomplishments which guaranteed them a particular identity or experience; rather, they had to constantly be monitored and repeated. This required a high level of vigilance, patrolling what Goffman calls the Umwelt, 'the region around which the signs for alarm can come' (1971: 297). They had to be ready to repair their own failed transgressions or mistakes, such as the one Laura describes here:

> There was one time when I went out for a meal with my mum and dad and my sister and instead of pouring vinegar on my chips I actually poured the water from the flower vase on my chips. I could hear everyone stop eating and they were all looking at me, thinking 'what a shame', I could tell. I just wanted to disappear. The only thing I could do was burst out laughing then everyone else did as well.

She said the looks were coming, not from her family, but from other people in the restaurant, but her family did nothing until she rescued them by laughing. This erased the immediate pity which she sensed they felt for her, yet left them with a feeling of admiration for the way her humour 'saw her through' difficult moments.

Raschida described a kind of solidarity among her visually impaired friends:

> I find that if I go out with other partially sighted girls from the unit, they seem to laugh about the thing. If I go out with my big sister or my pals and if I do something stupid, sometimes they just totally ignore it and pretend it never happened and just continue on. It's just that people react differently.

She described how an outing was successful as the result of planning and team work:

> The day I went to Edinburgh I was with a blind girl and she was with a guy who has a sight problem, but his is really good sight just now. But she got the train to Central and we were supposed to meet, I was supposed to meet her and the guy, but I hadn't seen the guy before and he hadn't seen me, but I told him I'd meet them at this place, then they came and we found each other and then I told them what platform the train was and then when we reached Edinburgh, the guy, he found our way out of Edinburgh station and we got a taxi and that was it.

There are two interesting points here: the first is the hierarchy of sightedness she invokes, in which they all pull together, but where more is expected of the person with the best sight; the second point relates to the temporal nature of the hierarchy in which the 'guy' has 'really good sight, just now', but with the suggestion that things could change. This could relate to her own recent experience of deteriorating vision or to a more general stance on disability, such as those taken by disabled rights activists, who use the term TAB to describe non-disabled people as 'temporarily able bodied' (Shapiro, 1993: 35). On a different occasion Raschida was surprised to find how one of the girls from the unit had behaved when a group of them went out together:

> Sharon's got the best sight of all of us and she was so . . . bitchy towards me because I couldn't see and instead of warning me that there was something coming up she would just walk away and she was in a huff all the time, but when I'm with my fully sighted friends it's just so different and I would have thought it would have been the other way round. The other (visually impaired) girls were fine about it, I don't know what it is, it's just put me off going out with them.

Raschida seemed to feel let down by Sharon, who might have been more supportive, but who apparently chose not to. Sharon, in this instance, appeared to be acting as a coercive threat to Raschida's transgressive efforts.

Barry

The transgression practised by Barry, a wheelchair user, involved 'holding on', in order to avoid the fuss associated with going to the toilet at school. This involved hoisting him from his wheelchair onto the toilet and Barry preferred to wait until he got home. Using the toilet appeared to be a coercive marker of disability which Barry sought to avoid. Outside school, another coercive marker had come through his mother's fund-raising efforts, creating a spectacle of his disability. His mainstream peers paid little attention to him, and were therefore neither collusive agents nor coercive markers of disability. He did, however, seek to influence their neutrality by keeping his head down in class, working hard and avoiding drawing attention to his disability.

Barry said he hated anyone fussing over him. He found that people either made him the focus of attention or ignored him, speaking to the auxiliary who accompanied him throughout the school day as if he wasn't there. A large sum of money had been raised recently to buy him a special bed, and his mother was about to be given a van which would hold his wheelchair. The trouble with this was the endless publicity, including a television appearance, which he had to endure and which he found abhorrent. Much to his relief, his mother had begun to see his point of view and had refused further publicity. Barry said he was friendly with two pupils, a boy and a girl, who acted as his 'helpers' during intervals and lunchtimes. He said he would have preferred to go home for lunch, but was not allowed. He had only recently been allowed to visit the shop at lunchtime and to eat on his own: 'they don't let me out of their sight, even at intervals. I don't know what they think I'm going to do.'

Barry appeared to resist identification of himself as disabled, especially where this might draw attention to himself. Although he could control this by avoiding trips to the toilet during the day, he needed help with some things, for example, getting lunch. Within the classroom, he tried to escape the gaze of teachers and peers by being a diligent pupil who needed little help other than with some physical tasks. Barry said he worked hard in the mainstream classroom (where he spent all of his time) so that he would do as well as any other pupil and 'stop people feeling sorry for me'. He said his teacher 'didn't need to do anything special' for him, although his auxiliary usually helped him with writing, 'which can be a bit slow sometimes'. Her main function was to help him with the toilet, but he said he tried to hold on during the day as it was a 'bit awkward'. He said he had not minded being helped to go to the toilet when he was younger, but now he had to be 'hoisted' onto the toilet and he would prefer not to have the 'hassle'. The auxiliary worried about the effects this could have on his health, but she understood his embarrassment and had to accept his decision.

Barry's attempts at removing pity by working hard and 'holding on' to avoid embarrassing situations suggests a considerable degree of agency. The implications of the latter of these transgressions for his health, however, are significant and he had already experienced some stomach problems. He seemed to reinforce a neutrality in the eyes of his peers and this seemed to make him uninteresting to the majority of them, at least according to his friend: 'There's people (sic) who don't take much interest in him. They sometimes don't pay a lot of attention to him. But most people are nice to him.' Barry's attempts at transgressing his disabled identity, then, could be interpreted as both a success and a failure. He succeeded by avoiding the attention of his peers and, in a sense, eroded their need to govern their conduct towards him. Yet, he also failed by creating a disinterested gaze which seemed to disconnect him from them.

Transgressing into Disability

Susan

Susan's efforts seemed to be directed towards transgressing into a disabled identity, seeking out those coercive markers of disability which appeared so threatening to Raschida, Laura and Barry. For Susan, these markers took the form of her electric wheelchair, which made her more 'special' than other physically disabled youngsters in the school, a visit by government officials and fundraising activities associated with a trip to the Peto institute. Unlike Barry, Susan valued such events in which her disability was given prominence. Her mainstream peers acted as co-conspirators in the process of transgressing into disability, praising her dependence on them and her willingness to ask them for help and she in turn reinforced this view among them. Susan's teachers provided the biggest threat to her transgressive efforts, by urging her to become less dependent and passive and discouraging mainstream pupils from making a fuss of her. The coercive markers of disability which her teachers laid down were associated with accepting the limitations of her disability and learning independence skills (Chapter 5).

'One good thing about being in a wheelchair is that you get to meet lots of people', said Susan, listing the 'important people' who had been to see her. She said she had been in the newspapers, as part of publicity to raise money for a trip to the Peto Institute in Hungary. She described the attention she received as wonderful, which contrasts with Barry's response to coercive markers of disability of this kind. She had also been the focus of a visit from the Scottish Home and Health Department, initiated by her mother in a bid to secure physiotherapy provision for her. According to the headteacher, she had 'wrapped them around her little finger' and they had been 'absolutely captivated by her'. A physiotherapist had been provided a few days after the visit. 'People will always do things for me because they know I can't walk', she said. Susan's transgression seemed to be to seek identification as a kind of disabled 'star', although, as Shapiro (1993) notes, this is an oppressive view which is located within charity discourses.

Susan spent some of her time in a special unit along with pupils with physical and cognitive disabilities. She also participated in mainstream classes and it was there that Susan worked on her disabled identity for the audience of her mainstream peers. As a celebrity figure, she was made welcome and fussed over whenever she went into the mainstream classroom, despite efforts by the class teacher to prevent this. She created an obligation among her mainstream peers to help her and they responded positively to her dependence on them, commending her ability to rely upon them and ask them for help. Susan reinforced this by allowing them to take some responsibility for her progress, as the following exchange she had with a pupil suggests:

S   I can't read your writing.
G   No, it's not very clear is it?

The mainstream pupils seemed willing to accept some responsibility for Susan's progress and to alter any of their own behaviour which might restrict this:

G   I think [Susan] found that my writing wasn't exactly neat.
JA   Is that right? Do you think your writing wasn't neat?
G   No it's not really.
J   Mine's sometimes not neat.
G   I was in a bit of a hurry at the time.
J   Yeah, we were rushing, because we didn't have it finished.
JA   So what happened, when Susan didn't find your writing neat?
G   She was stuttering on the words and she was asking, what's that word and what does that say?
JA   And what did you do?
G   Well I just helped her.
J   On the second time through, we gave her the book instead to make it easier.

Susan's policing of her own identity involved maintaining her visibility as a disabled person, standing out from others in the school with physical disabilities. She spoke of how she felt her status within the school and her self-image had suddenly been threatened when another member of the unit was given an electric wheelchair. Until then she had been the only one with a wheelchair of this kind and said 'it makes me a bit special — [mainstream pupils] make jokes about it, asking me how fast I can go in it'. Teachers described how 'furious' she had been when the other pupil received his wheelchair. 'It took a lot for her to admit it but she finally said to me, "I'm actually jealous of Alan".' Susan seemed to view the second wheelchair as a threat to those transgressive actions which enabled her to stand out from the other disabled pupils. She still had an advantage over the other pupil, however, as he did not participate in mainstream classes, where she did most of her transgressive work.

Peter

Peter's transgression was, like Susan's, into a disabled identity. His official label of emotional or behavioural difficulties had been contended by his father who argued that Peter was no worse than himself as a boy. For Peter, the absence of outward signs of disability meant a lack of sympathy, particularly from his mainstream peers. Their pedagogic strategies were aimed at a kind of normalization, by ignoring his 'overboard' behaviour and involving him in class activities. Yet, he often appeared to them to be simply lazy or naughty, which tested the limits of their pastoral power by making them question the extent to which he deserved their 'special' treatment. Peter worked on this by seeking some coercive markers from another, more visible, disability and claimed incapacity on the grounds that he was a 'spastic'. His occasional bizarre behaviour, in which he threatened to kill himself or his mainstream peers might be explained in a similar vein, as an attempt to work on his mainstream peers' perceptions of him as (more) disabled. Peter's teachers threatened his transgressive efforts by pathologizing them as another indicator of his emotional or behavioural difficulties and suggesting that his parents had prompted this response (Chapter 5).

'I sometimes say things to shock people', said Peter. 'Like I tell them I'm going to kill myself but I don't mean it.' In the past, he had opted out of activities at school and home, claiming that he couldn't do them because he was a 'spastic'. According to his mother, this seemed to occur when he sensed a lack of sympathy for his behavioural problems from his mainstream peers:

> There was a while when he had this thing about being a spastic, you know. 'I can't do that, pick my cup up because I'm a spastic.' You know you ask someone to pass over something — 'I can't do that I'm spastic' 'I can't feed the rabbit, I'm spastic', I think because he was being teased at school.

Peter may have picked up the notion that children were more favourably regarded if they had a discernible impairment, and so tried to acquire one. His classmates seemed disposed towards excusing his behaviour or giving him the benefit of the doubt. Peter spent about a third of his week in mainstream and the remainder in the school's special unit. He did his transgressive work in both settings, although his mainstream teacher thought he only behaved 'over the top' in the special unit. According to his peers, he seemed mostly to respond to their governmental regime, in which they sought to reinforce normal behaviour and discourage his bizarre actions. However, they indicated that he occasionally lost control and started behaving oddly.

They could influence this to a certain extent, by restricting his input to group activities and ignoring him when he went 'overboard', but could identify situations where he was likely to behave badly and over which they would have no control. For example, they speculated on how Peter would respond to the task of wiring a light bulb:

J   Watch out!
[All laugh]
JA   What do you think will happen?
C   Bang!
J   He'll probably try his best and try to do it.
B   He'll probably start messing around, but if you tell him to stop messing around he'll stop.
C   Or he might not do anything at all.
P   Yeah he might just sit and watch.
K   He'll probably ask a few questions about how to do it and if you don't know, you'll say 'I don't know' and he'll say, 'but how?' so you can't really explain it properly, that that's what we're trying to find out.

The pupils seemed to believe that he would participate and that he would 'probably try his best and try to do it', but they also had strong doubts that he would do anything at all. Peter's transgressions, then, seemed to occur when his participation in mainstream was demanding and may have served as a kind of personal rescue.

Two-way Transgression

Phillip

Phillip's transgressive practices appeared to be ambivalent and were directed both away from and towards disability. They generally involved attempts to remain mobile, but these were becoming increasingly difficult as his muscular dystrophy progressed and occasionally Phillip sought comfort in visible markers of disability such as a wheelchair and walking sticks. These were the only coercive elements, as his mainstream peers conspired to help retain normality by picking him up whenever he fell and making light of it. His teachers recognized the coercive measures which lay ahead for Phillip, in the form of a wheelchair and the need to choose an accessible secondary school. However, they worked with Phillip to keep these away for as long as possible and, unusually, allowed Phillip's desires to guide their practice.

Phillip began his school career like any other ambulant 5-year-old. His condition emerged as he went through primary and he said that by the time he was properly diagnosed as having muscular dystrophy, he was relieved that there was an explanation for the difficulties he had been having, as he had been saying to himself, 'Look, I'm trying to do all these things to walk properly, but I'm not.' His parents had constantly nagged him to walk properly and he had tried. Now that there was a reason for being unable to do so, he said he felt he had been 'let off the hook'. At the time of the research, he was able to walk with the use of sticks, but often fell over and had to be picked up by his peers. Phillip indicated that he managed to cope well at present, but his disability was likely to get worse and there were going to be greater demands on him as he got older in any case. Secondary school, for example, would involve much more walking around than in primary and he worried about what lay ahead. 'I sometimes wonder how I'm going to do all the things you have to manage when you're older.' Phillip suggested that people expected too much of him because he did not look particularly disabled. 'Just because I look alright people think I can do things but if you're in a wheelchair, you know something's wrong.' This might be interpreted as a transgression into, rather than out of, a disabled identity in which recognition of this by others could make life less demanding.

Although Phillip sought some comfort in these markers of disability, most of his transgressive efforts were directed away from disability. He said he wanted to be treated normally and to do all the things his classmates did. He was pleased, he said, that he was clever and was in the top group for all subjects. He tried to plan ahead, so that he did not find himself in difficult situations. For instance, as a member of the school quiz team, he travelled to another school, but checked beforehand that he would be able to get onto the stage before the other pupils arrived. There seemed to be a tacit agreement between Phillip and his peers within the classroom or the playground to ignore his disability; this was only challenged whenever he fell over. These episodes tended to be very short lived, in which the mainstream pupils 'just yank him up and make a laugh of it' and appeared not to challenge his usual identification as 'one of the boys'. His headteacher mentioned a very close friend who 'very unobtrusively looks after him and other children who are prepared to do that'.

Phillip's transgression initially took the form of resistance to certain kinds of help, but this changed as his condition developed. The headteacher described how she allowed him to make these decisions:

> It took him a while to talk to me about the help he'd need. I would take the children with mobility problems to church, but Phillip resisted that for a while until, in his own time, he decided it would be helpful to him to be driven. The same with the bus — the step is too big, so it was decided he would walk to meet his dad — a few tumbles. He still won't accept the taxi, which he could do with, but he himself is not ready for it.

His mainstream peers had been asked 'not to run to help him every time, because he preferred that', but a point had been reached where 'we're now beyond that because when he goes down he can't get up'. This did not, however, seem remarkable to the mainstream pupils, since 'if he falls or something, people will help him' and a group of four pupils walked him home from school each day 'in case he falls'. The only noteworthy feature of this for the pupils was that one of them was capable of picking Phillip up all by himself.

Transgression and New Forms of Subjectivity

The practices of the six pupils appeared to be transgressive, in that they challenged the fixed identity (usually as disabled) and the limits imposed by this. Their actions did not involve complete rejection of particular identities, nor transcendence of limits, but a much more playful and unstable contest, with actions such as refusal, trickery or pretence. Raschida, Laura and Barry's practices were directed at transgressing out of the disabled identity, while Sarah and Peter's efforts seem to be focused in the opposite direction, towards disability. In each of these cases, transgression was not a singular act, but had to be constantly repeated and required vigilance from the pupils. The pupils had to practise their transgression under the threat of coercive markers of disability which constrained them to behave as disabled people, but these seemed to be valuable commodities for Susan and Peter. Phillip's transgressive actions were much more ambivalent. With the help of his peers and his teachers, he was able, mostly, to transgress the disability which was progressively restricting his mobility. At the same time, however, knowledge that he had a disability had provided a certain comfort, since it explained why he had found so many things difficult. He had occasionally wished his disability was more visible, for example confining him to a wheelchair, because people might be more sympathetic. Transgression out of disability was, for Phillip, desirable, but it was hard work and so was practised with a backward glance. Mainstream pupils, within their mini-regime of governmentality, acted as fellow tricksters, colluding with the pupils' efforts at transgression, both in and out of disability. Occasionally, however, they acted as coercive markers of disability, by being 'uptight', in Raschida and Laura's case, or in Peter's case by being suspicious of the extent of his disability. In an attempt to remove these markers, Raschida and Laura worked at educating their peers out of their discomfort, whereas Peter provided confirmation of a disability by going 'over the top' and affecting incapacity.

The kind of otherness attained through transgression was fragmented, liminal and never complete. It required, therefore, an acute self-awareness in which the pupils had to 'oscillate between being off guard and on guard' (Goffman, 1971: 287), repairing acts of indiscretion by themselves and others. Each of the transgressions had their own efficacy, allowing individuals to do work on themselves and their mainstream peers. The actions of Raschida and Laura seemed to have been particularly effective, going by their peers' accounts of how they had become less 'uptight' and had come to behave in ways with which the girls felt comfortable.

Barry had created a kind of social invisibility for himself, which seemed to have both positive and negative effects, whereas Susan and her peers seemed pleased with her dependence. Phillip appeared to have benefited from the collusive agency of both his peers and teachers in helping him to retain mobility for as long as possible. Yet, transgression is a risky activity and the final part of this chapter explores the hazards involved.

The Art of Living Dangerously

Transgression carries certain risks for individuals, primarily because it involves rejecting (though not entirely) the limits imposed by others. The first danger is that those who set the limits, in this case teachers, might be affronted by the challenge. This was indeed the reaction by Raschida and Laura's teachers, who judged their transgressive practices as a 'failure' to accept their disability or a lack of cooperation. Barry's headteacher bemoaned the waste of money on a toilet which he didn't use, whereas Susan's teachers were highly critical of what they saw as an unwillingness to accept their goal of independence. Peter's teachers indicated that his claim on a more discernible disability simply confirmed the existence of his emotional or behavioural problems. Phillip's teachers were exceptional in colluding with his transgression and allowing his desires, rather than his needs, to guide their practice. The teachers made their views clear in their negative reports about these practices, in which they prophesied educational failure if such transgressive practices were continued. Their responses to transgression are explored more fully in Chapter 5.

Transgression enables individuals to acquire new forms of subjectivity, but there is a risk that these may not be the ones the individual desires. For example, Laura's repair of her failed transgression in which she poured water, instead of vinegar, on her chips, erased the immediate silence and pity which she sensed from her family and onlookers. However, it left them full of admiration at her ability to laugh at herself, which Shapiro (1993) suggests is another version of pity. Raschida found that transgressing her visual impairment led to a new set of problems. Her school friends did not appreciate the difficulties she had out of school and the problems of travel because she appeared so competent at making her way around school. She said she tried to make excuses not to see them outside the school:

> Because I don't live here it takes me an hour to get from my house to here and then from here to wherever they're going. Because I live so far I've only been out no more than four times . . . and my mum doesn't like me going on the trains on my own. So it's quite difficult and I always try and think of excuses why I can't go. But I usually tell them it's because of transport. And some of them have just learnt to drive so they're offering 'can I come and pick you up?'

On other occasions Raschida had been so successful in avoiding 'drawing attention to [her] eyes', for example during evenings out, that she then became reluctant to 'spoil things' by doing anything that would 'remind people' of her disability. Barry's reluctance to use the toilet during the day was understandable, given that it involved an undignified use of a 'hoist' and the assistance of his female special needs auxiliary. Yet he may have been storing up health problems for himself in the future, which could be exacerbated when he moved to secondary school.

As Foucault (1977c) points out, the effort to go beyond limits reveals the limits, but can paradoxically reinforce them. This may be frustrating for individuals for whom the act of transgressing their disabled identity may make them more aware of the impossibility of transcending this or changing their material circumstances. Berman argues that such awareness is nevertheless valuable, since 'once we grasp the total futility of it all, at least we can relax' (1982: 34). Others have suggested that knowledge of one's limits, even where there is little possibility of changing these, can be empowering. Collins, for example, writing about black American women, argues that they have become empowered through change occurring 'in the private, personal space of an individual woman's consciousness . . . even within conditions that severely limit one's ability to act' (1991: 111). Lorde, on the other hand, argues for a better connection between agency and self-understanding, insisting that 'our acts against oppression become integral with self, motivated and empowered from within' (1982: 58). There is a difficulty in reconciling transgressive actions by individuals with collective empowerment and social change, since it requires simultaneously resisting an identity and mobilizing around it (Deleuze, 1997). Pupils can, however, be encouraged to do work on themselves which allows them to identify goals, scrutinize the limits to achieving these goals and determine individual or collective actions which either challenge or accept these limits. This is explored in the final chapter.

Chapter 5

In Need of Support?
Transgression and the Teacher

Teachers seemed to present the greatest challenge to the pupils' transgressive practices by subjugating their desires beneath professionally expressed 'needs'. The specialist and mainstream teachers who worked with Raschida, Laura, Susan, Barry and Peter were either unaware of the significance of their strategies or saw them as counter-productive to the support they were offering. Even Raschida and Laura's mainstream peers commented on their teachers' insensitivity to the girls' desire to be 'treated normally'. Phillip's teachers and Barry's auxiliary seemed to be the only people to recognize the value of their transgressions, yet still problematized them as acts which masked their 'true feelings' or created negative consequences. This chapter examines the teachers' readings of the pupils' practices which, in Chapter 4 were interpreted as transgressive, but for the teachers stood in the way of the support they were trying to offer. Raschida's practices were read, not as transgressions (successful or otherwise), but as evidence of her failure to accept her impairment and the support they could offer. Laura seemed to receive less criticism because she was more 'cooperative' and her teachers also acknowledged her attempts to transgress her disabled identity. Susan's efforts at cultivating a kind of obligation among her peers were simply indefensible in the eyes of staff, who were seeking to encourage her to be independent. Peter's claim that he was a 'spastic' and his other 'bizarre' behaviour were pathologized as arising from low self-esteem and other failings, including those of his parents. The teachers' readings of the pupils' transgressive practices, for example, as failures to 'come to terms' with or accept what they considered inevitable restrictions imposed by disability, appeared to contradict and threatened to undo some of them. The teachers, however, were responding within a professional discourse which privileged special needs over the desires of individual pupils and these can be understood as part of the multi-layered discourses operating within the classroom.

Coming to Terms with Disability

Raschida's specialist teachers were critical of her for failing to 'accept' her impairment and noted this in a review of her Record of Needs:

> Raschida is being extremely difficult about accepting that she requires help and is trying to pretend to be able to read print which we are aware is too small or too

obscure. However, she does not like to fail and we are hoping that she will come to appreciate . . . that she must accept support in order to succeed.

Chapter 6 examines in more detail the role of the Record of Needs, the Scottish equivalent of a statement, as a disciplinary technique. In this functionalist view of disability, Raschida was being constrained to fail in her attempts at normality and to succeed as disabled. Raschida's teachers repeated the tale told by Raschida in Chapter 4 of how she dropped her long cane in the lake, as an illustration of the 'difficulty she had in accepting her disability'. Her teachers also described the period when her eyesight deteriorated as one in which there was 'a lot of weeping and wailing and gnashing of teeth' and where 'she was resistant to the idea of learning Braille'. They viewed her as reluctant to undertake something which signalled for her a passage into the world of the 'blind'. One teacher, however, said she 'eventually came to realize that she couldn't just rely on us for tapes and to read for her'.

Laura's teachers were more positive about her 'attitude to her impairment' and wrote 'In all respects, Laura is a normal girl. Her parents and teachers will continue to ensure she maintains her relaxed and balanced attitude towards her visual impairment . . . She is independent, but able to accept help which she needs.' They acknowledged the significance of her transgressive practices, but sanctioned these only in so far as they did not exceed her 'limitations'. 'Her mobility is good in that she sensibly stays with the limitations imposed by the severity of her VI. However, she does this so skilfully that there are few apparent differences between Laura and her peers.' Laura's actions could be read as transgressive, yet the teachers regarded it as vanity, on a par with concern over spots or a wearing a brace on her teeth; they also undermined Laura's gender and sexual identity by discouraging vain behaviour (Chapter 8). The pupils' refusal to undergo mobility training where they might be seen by their friends posed problems for their teachers, since 'the point of the training' was to teach them 'independence in their home environment'.

The pupils' attempts to act 'normally' were challenged in the mainstream classrooms by the specialist teachers who came to support them. The teachers helped only those with visual impairment and often sat beside them to do so. Specialist staff said this was 'a bit of a shame', but inevitable if they were to provide the necessary help, for example, reading aloud to pupils. One teacher commented on how she had 'not minded' a mainstream pupil sitting beside Raschida, but in the end the constant talk between Raschida and the teacher proved too distracting for the pupil, who moved to another seat. She described a compromise the previous year:

> It was the Higher and it was her and her brother both in the same class and I sat in the middle and at one point we had Abdul's friend sitting with us, so we had four desks all put together, so it wasn't very practical, but I wouldn't put a stop to it because I think it's really good if they do have friends sitting beside them. And the other kids, they really are very good, most of them. They're maybe not totally aware of all their problems, but they're quite understanding. They'll read things out from the board and help them.

This appears to challenge Raschida's efforts at behaving 'normally' in mainstream. The teacher said she 'wouldn't put a stop' to her brother's friend 'sitting with us', implying it was a hindrance, yet acknowledged the social benefits. She also described the mainstream pupils as 'quite understanding' and helpful, which suggests a lack of awareness of their nuanced understanding of disability and of their governmental regime.

One of Raschida's strategies in maths, at which she was very able, was to do as many of the operations as possible in her head. There was little point, she said, in writing things down because she could not then read them. The teachers, however, tried to thwart this. In examinations, pupils must show their calculations and teachers did everything they could to encourage her to do this to ensure her success. Beyond that, however, her mathematical talents were problematized within the teachers' functionalist discourse. A maths teacher who had taught her in the past remarked upon the 'great shame' that Raschida did not write down her 'workings'. A specialist teacher accompanied her to each maths class and acted as an amanuensis for her or read aloud anything she had written. In other classes, Raschida was encouraged to use the Braille machine, similar to a very loud typewriter. Laura seemed to 'manage' with 'raised diagrams' and enlarged versions of resources used by mainstream pupils. All of these devices, which the teachers saw as important forms of support for the pupils, often acted as coercive markers of disability and threatened the girls' transgressive efforts.

Raschida and Laura said that their teachers were more uncomfortable than their mainstream peers with their visual impairment. Raschida, for example, mentioned a student teacher's attempt to avoid the taboo associated with seeing/not seeing:

> She's really nice, but she never says 'see' to me — she says 'I'll give you this and you can listen to it' and it's a sheet of paper and she never likes to use the word 'see', or anything to do with the eyes and you can tell when people are trying to avoid that. It puts you off.

Raschida thought this was amusing and indicative of the embarrassment her impairment had caused. She drew parallels with a famous television sketch from *Fawlty Towers*, in which Basil Fawlty is told that a party of Germans are visiting his hotel and warned not to mention the war, but ends up goose-stepping before them. Both girls found most teachers drew attention to their impairment, for example, by checking that they were able to see something properly, but said that this was often unnecessary. Some teachers went 'over the top' in their efforts to be as helpful as possible:

> They always ask you to come down to the front, in front of the whole class and things like that and I don't really need to be at the front because I can't see the board in the first place anyway and if it's television, I prefer sitting at the back, because I've got tunnel vision and I can see it better. (Raschida)

Raschida's comment illustrates the paradox of inclusion for her: the teachers, by trying to help her, were disabling her by making it more difficult to see and drawing attention to her impairment.

The mainstream pupils in Raschida and Laura's classes accused their teachers of being highly insensitive, by drawing attention to the girls' impairment needlessly. They thought this occurred where teachers felt sorry for them, but said that this was the wrong attitude to have towards them. Laura's friend commented on the inappropriateness of grouping her with other visually impaired pupils for the convenience of providing support, because it made her feel embarrassed. Another pupil mentioned a teacher who was very patronizing towards two visually impaired pupils:

> She was going on about the fact that they couldn't see properly, she just kept going on and on, and just wouldn't stop. If you ask Marie she'll tell you, because Marie told her mum and dad and they said just don't do anything, just wait and see if she does it again, because she didn't want to stir anything up. She was being really really bad, because I'm in Marie's English class. She was being really really horrible to her and Gaphar.

Laura's peers also accused the teachers of giving her unnecessary 'special treatment':

> I think they sometimes go out of their way to help her, but she doesn't like that, she likes to be treated normally. She much prefers to be treated normally. She doesn't like any special treatment . . . I think she likes to be treated normally. If anybody makes a fuss of her she gets really embarrassed and she just doesn't like it. She's always complaining if people make a fuss of her. She'll say, 'Oh God, I wish they hadn't done that.' She just likes to be treated like everyone else.

The phrase 'treated normally' is interesting because it implies that they are not considered normal in the ontological sense, that is, their being or essence is not regarded as normal. One of Laura's peers suggested that supply teachers usually made the biggest fuss because 'they don't know about her [and] they maybe make allowances or whatever'.

The mainstream pupils were highly critical of teachers who singled Raschida, Laura or any other pupils with visual impairment out for 'special treatment' or paid them too much attention because they understood the challenge they represented to their transgressive actions. Laura received the ultimate accolade from her friend for resisting such behaviour publicly:

> For instance, there was one time, people were talking in class, it was, like, a group of us, just girls in my group and one of them was talking to Laura and so one of them got a punishment exercise and Laura didn't, because she's visually impaired. So Laura spoke up and said, 'I'd like one too — there's no point in treating me differently, because I don't like that, I just want to be treated normally.' So some teachers are like that and others just treat her normally and I think she prefers that.

And she doesn't like getting separated, like they put the [pupils with visual impairment] all in a group and she doesn't like that, she likes to sit where she wants to sit and if she wants help they can help her. She doesn't like to get separated . . . she thinks that's embarrassing.

Barry did not have the same level of classroom support as Raschida and Laura, but had an auxiliary with him throughout the day. As far as classwork was concerned, his mainstream teacher had 'no problems with him' and thought he had accepted his disability. 'He doesn't feel sorry for himself, unlike some wheelchair bound children. He just gets on with things and enjoys life.' Barry's physical difficulties had not proved to be a problem to his class teacher, beyond having to make a few adjustments:

Obviously he has to have bigger spaces provided for him in certain areas — he can't just slip through a normal space so you have really got to think big in all aspects so that he can come round with the whole class . . . trying to overcome the mobility problems or difficulties with space. Otherwise, it's just giving him the same curriculum experiences as other children. His condition does not really concern my work with him in class as it doesn't affect it.

Barry's main difficulty, as far as his teacher was concerned, was his unwillingness to go to the toilet during the day. She recognized that this was a 'sensitive area' for him, but explained the practical problems involved. 'He doesn't even use the bottle she has for him, just holds out till he gets home. His auxiliary would find it difficult to lift him in any case and there isn't the proper equipment for her in the school.'

The headteacher took a rather more parsimonious view of Barry's reticence, saying that, having spent £1800 to adapt a toilet for his use, he regretted the fact that 'he never goes'. Barry's auxiliary gave an account of assisting him to use the toilet:

I've got a pump hoist and he does get heavy sometimes when you're pumping Barry up and down . . . If I've got him in the hoist I've got this arm trying to guide him back to make sure he's not getting [part of his wheelchair] in his ribs and I'm leaning over trying to work the hoist to get him down.

It was little wonder, she mused, that he was reluctant to be manoeuvred in such a way:

He's never wanted to go to the toilet since I've been here . . . He uses a bottle and we asked his mum about putting [trousers with] flies on and she did at first but then she stopped it. So if he needed the toilet [another auxiliary] and I would have to actually lift him onto the bed, get his things down for him to use the bottle on the bed. I think that probably puts him off a bit and I think we're going to have to get that sorted before [secondary school] . . . I don't think the toileting's ideal at all . . . That's the thing that worries me most. Not physically doing it but getting it so that Barry's not embarrassed and the time it would take to do it. Up in the [secondary school] there might not even be another auxiliary. I know that in fire regulations they say a janitor comes but I don't think Barry would like a janitor helping me to toilet him.

The auxiliary expressed her anxiety that Barry would lose confidence in her because 'we couldn't get things done in time'. Meanwhile she found his reluctance to 'be toileted' perfectly understandable, at the same time worrying about the effects of this on his health.

Independently Disabled

Susan's mainstream peers, it was suggested in Chapter 4, praised her dependence on them. Her class teacher, however, took a rather different view:

> When she first comes in, they make a big fuss and ask 'can she sit at our table?' and I have to say 'look Susan is part of the class, she's not here to be made a fuss of, she's here to come in and be treated as . . .' [pauses] you know . . . There's a few of them there that like to mother her and Susan likes that you know. Susan sits back and lets them mother her and you've got to try and get away from that and onto the idea that she's got to do things independently.

Her teacher said her ambition would ultimately encourage her to be independent, but according to her specialist teacher, she was inclined to ask others for help, rather than do things by herself. 'Her own personality can be a barrier — it's a double edged sword, because she won't sit back and not get. She'll ask and she'll make friends and enemies that way.'

Susan's headteacher described her as a 'child who likes attention' and the specialist teacher questioned whether her experience of being in a special unit had discouraged her independence and her perceptions of her own abilities:

> I think that the fact that she's been segregated . . . has led her to not be really aware of some things. She has a warped sense of what she's able to do. When it comes to putting thoughts down on paper I think she's able to do more than she thinks she can and at the same time her maths aren't that great, but I think she has an inflated idea of her maths . . . getting her out into mainstream will hopefully sort that out.

Her teachers considered themselves to be challenging Susan and her parents, who, they felt, had a misguided notion about what was best for her, emphasizing physical rehabilitation in favour of academic progress. The specialist teacher was particularly critical of Susan's mother:

> She has this narrow view of the physical needs and that is what she fought so hard for . . . [Susan] has to try and maintain whatever physical level she's reached but she's never going to be on her feet. She's at the stage now where she can be functioning at the same as the other children in the mainstream and she has to

get that because that's where her future lies. It's not in getting independently walking . . . I know they do a lot at home, but if [her mum] had got away from this fixation of the school [physiotherapist], I think we might have had Susan in the same physical state as she is today but maybe further on in some of her attainments.

Susan and her mother had been instrumental in obtaining much needed physiotherapy for the school and the headteacher described the episode with some ambivalence:

Her mother became concerned at the lack of physiotherapy in the school and she opened up a legal case with the Scottish Office and we ended up with various Inspectorate inquiries and visits and so on over a period of months, although there was a high point when we had a deputation from the Scottish Office who came and visited us. It was great — Susan absolutely wrapped them round her little finger; they were absolutely captivated by her. That was a wee bit of a highlight if you like and as a result there was an improvement in the provision of physiotherapy. The mother is a particularly forceful person which was quite interesting.

Criticism of Susan's tendency to 'sit back' was recorded officially in her Record of Needs: 'Participation in the wider activities of the school is important and a reasonable degree of firmness will be required to discourage Susan from being too dependent on others.' In her school report, Susan was described as a 'charming little girl, with an assured manner' which she used 'to control situations and avoid demands being placed on her'. Her parents were criticized for finding it difficult 'to make adequate demands' on her, and the teachers resolved to push her towards greater independence. 'The staff are looking for Susan to initiate more action rather than waiting for someone to see to her needs and are following the dressing programme suggested by the [occupational therapist].'

The specialist teacher was anxious that she would not be sufficiently independent to cope with mainstream secondary school, but still hoped that she could be helped to catch up. Indeed they noted some good signs, including a positive attitude towards, and acceptance of, her disability:

On occasions [when] she has been frustrated by her disability, she has been able to express feelings openly. Through discussion with adults [she has been] helped to deal with problems. [She has a] mature approach to life . . . Susan has a fighting spirit and copes well with difficulties and problems. She talks through her problems and meets new challenges in good spirit.

Susan's classroom teacher described how, as a newly qualified teacher, she had to learn how to leave her to work on her own, despite wanting to give her lots of attention:

I'm very aware of the fact that she's not there to be set out, you know, to stand out, to get individual attention and that's something I had to learn myself, that I had to draw back and leave her to work independently . . . I would like to do more for her, but I want to draw back and give her a realistic taste of what it is like to be in a mainstream classroom.

The teacher felt she had succeeded, much to her own satisfaction and to their mutual benefit. 'I want integration for as many activities as possible — it's a shame if she misses out in being part of the class. It's important that when she comes into the class that she is treated as normally as possible . . . Susan to me has been a challenge that's paid off.' Despite her obvious pleasure at what she had accomplished, the idea of Susan being completely integrated, as a full time member of the class, seemed an impossibility. 'It would be nice if Susan could come through more of the time. I would like Susan in more or less full time . . . It would be nice to have her as a more permanent member of the class, but I don't know how that works. [I don't understand] the school system.'

Susan's teachers saw her transgressive actions as posing a direct threat to her achievement of independence. They gave no indication of seeking to understand other possible motives behind her practices, for example, as a means of cultivating affection among her peers or as a response to the inability of others to deal with her disability (Sinason, 1992). Instead, staff had dismissed them as countermanding their own incontrovertible goal of independence. Susan's jealous reaction to the 'competition' from another electric wheelchair user was seen as illustrating a conceit which they sought to discourage in her own interest.

Personal Pathologies

Peter's bizarre behaviour was only apparent to his teachers when he was in the special unit. His mainstream classmates, however, had witnessed such behaviour when he was with them. His teachers and his mother had observed a tendency for him to refer to himself as a 'spastic' or 'handicapped', engage in highly crude behaviour or threaten to commit suicide. Peters' teachers read his adoption of a disabled label, not as an act of transgression, but as something he had picked up from his parents. 'I feel that at home that is being said to him because a child doesn't pick that up about themselves, that they are handicapped, you know, using those kinds of words, so whether that's how they've punished him or taken out their own frustration on him, I don't know.'

His 'bizarre' behaviour was thought to be connected to his lack of self esteem and an inability to be accepted by his peers:

Peter is very anxious to be accepted and his own lack of self-respect and self-esteem hold him back; he is desperate to be liked and appear grown-up but he is unsure as to how to go about this — he is immature in this respect. He finds it difficult to conform to others' behaviour, therefore he tries to get others to be like him.

They emphasized, in both their written and verbal accounts, that 'all Peter's work is mood related' and therefore unpredictable. His teachers, as were Susan's, were anxious to help prepare him for his transfer to secondary school. This largely involved destroying his perception that he was 'handicapped' and improving his self-image. 'We're trying to prepare him as much as possible for going up to the academy . . . I think we're really talking about independence skills . . . he's got to be able to function properly, regardless of what his mum and dad have sown in his mind.'

His teachers also sought to reduce his other crude behaviour and considered offering him counselling, but thought exposure to mainstream classes was likely to be most useful:

> He has a home–school notebook for monitoring behaviour. The crudeness is dealt with as a serious issue . . . He would get more responsibility, maturity, if he went into mainstream more. It's a catch-22. The difficulty is in releasing staff to see if the familiarity with peers in mainstream is paying off . . . We do worry about the fact that in his efforts to get in with a group [in mainstream] he could be easily manipulated, you know, get in with the wrong crowd. The potential for that is really worrying and the fact that he's got this crudity as well, he'd be very easily manipulated.

As far as Peter's teachers were concerned, his odd behaviour, whether transgressive or not, largely disappeared when he went into mainstream classes. His classroom teacher had begun to question the validity of the specialist teachers' judgments:

> I'm told he has behavioural problems . . . 'Oh he's badly behaved and has problems.' I haven't seen any of that when he's been with me, you know he's always very keen and from the behavioural point of view that is excellent and I think he's come streets along the line of improving when he's with the children and with his peers in my class. I don't know why the difference. I wonder if it's because he's with his peers and he's been set tasks that he's really interested in, in which case that's really good.

His teacher had, however, 'seen what he's like in the base' and was mystified by the contrast between his behaviour in the two settings:

> You get snippets of insights; when I go into the [special unit] I see how he's been in my class and gone and immediately he's back he's started to be over the top again . . . He was showing off and using words he's never used in class — 'I'm going to electrocute myself' whereas he was being very sensible in the class. Then I went through and saw him being very silly with a very safe piece of equipment that is quite safe to use in the class . . . And I thought that was sad because everything he'd had positive in my class had immediately been knocked down and the teachers weren't seeing how good he'd been, you know, just from that switch.

This behaviour, which the class teacher claimed was absent from her own class, was, of course, well documented by the pupils (Chapters 3 and 4). Nevertheless, all staff agreed that exposing Peter to mainstream was highly beneficial. Indeed, the headteacher suggested that perhaps Peter should have been in mainstream all along. Peter's transgressions, then, seemed to signal to his teachers that they had merely got his placement decision wrong, rather than anything more significant.

Assisted Transgression

Phillip's teachers appeared, unusually, to recognize the significance of his transgressions. His classroom teacher referred to his obvious mobility difficulties and suggested that his peers would inevitably perceive these as getting worse. 'They're so used to Phillip getting slower and slower. I don't know if he's told them about his condition. He doesn't talk about it, but they might remember the wee boy who's now in a wheelchair — he used to be able to walk and they might link the two.'

The class teacher saw her task as trying to preserve 'normality' for as long as possible. 'Trying to make Phillip's life as normal as possible, to keep him integrated in the classroom.' She was assisted by Phillip's own efforts at avoiding difficult situations:

> Phillip asked not to take the book around the classes or to be sent messages — he doesn't like to do that. When we go to mass, he goes in the headteacher's car, because he can't manage the walk. When we have mass in the school, he likes to do a reading — he knows that's the only chance he can get, because he can't manage the steps up onto the altar.

Phillip, according to his class teacher, seemed to have accepted his own limitations and would opt out of particular activities — 'If there are things he can't do he just goes to the side.' There was plenty of evidence for her that, despite his worsening condition, 'his progress in relation to the rest of the class counts as proof that he's doing well'.

Phillip's headteacher was aware of how much knowledge he had of his condition:

> When he was first diagnosed as having muscular dystrophy, Phillip hadn't been told about it, but then the parents said they would talk to him. They decided not to tell him it was muscular dystrophy, but it quickly moved onto a decision that they would be much more frank with him.

As a consequence, Phillip had 'become very good at highlighting things that will be a problem for him. The teachers' goal of providing 'normality — not singling him out as different' was achieved by being 'one step ahead of anything that's happening [for example] in the classroom' without creating unnecessary fuss. 'We're certainly making sure access problems don't stop him here in [for example] taking part in the library quiz . . . we've just changed the format unobtrusively or strategically placed chairs.'

The headteacher acknowledged that the staff often got things wrong, since 'we don't always think of the ramifications for him', but either Phillip or his father would alert them to these, so any problems were usually resolved. Phillip, according to the headteacher, had taken some time to talk openly about the help he needed and was still reluctant to accept all that was available. The headteacher saw his decision to stop playing chess as regrettable, but understood it as a transgressive act. 'I think he might have dropped chess, feeling that his limitations were being set for him. We were disappointed because he was good and it was a cerebral task for him.'

Phillip's continued reluctance to accept taxi transportation became more problematic as his mobility problems increased, even though staff wanted to be guided by his readiness to accept help of this kind. Although he was praised for having a mature attitude towards his disability and for becoming 'less reluctant to accept help', it was noted that he exhibited no behavioural difficulties 'as yet'. This implied that staff anticipated such problems as his condition progressed. There was a considerable degree of collusion by staff to assist Phillip in his transgressions. Despite this, the headteacher worried about how Phillip was 'really coping' with his disability. She worried that his transgressive behaviour was masking his true feelings:

> I'd have to say I don't know the thoughts that are going through his head. I see him as coping very well and being very mature about it, but I don't know how much of that, to be honest, is a front and I don't know how much it takes out of him to present himself in that way . . . on occasions when he's not able to get up or when it causes, you know, just a wee bit of a spectacle . . . He seems to cope well with it and usually we can make a wee joke of it and he seems to shrug it off, but I don't know.

The headteacher's comments, expressing sympathy for Phillip's feelings about his condition, evoke a charity discourse which undermined the collusion of the staff in supporting Phillip's transgressions.

Teachers' Support: Needs or Desires?

The teachers' support focused on the pupils' disabilities and operated within a functionalist discourse, in which 'defect is located in the individual who becomes subject to classification, regulation and treatment' (Slee, 1998: 130). The pupils were required to perform their disability, through public acknowledgment, accepting help and abandoning or compromising their own transgressive projects. The teachers rationalized their judgments about pupils in terms of 'maturity' and 'sensible behaviour', at the same time erasing other aspects of adolescence, for example, by criticizing acts of 'vanity'. Yet there seemed to be no ideal type of disabled person, or 'docile body' which teachers held to and to which the pupils were expected to aspire. Consequently those pursuing independence (Raschida, Laura and Barry) and dependence (Susan) were criticized in equal measure, whereas Peters' attempt to switch disabilities was reduced to the pathological. Independence or self-advocacy is the frequently stated goal to which all pupils should aspire (Mittler, 1996; Oliver, 1988), even though the validity of this heuristic has been questioned (Corbett, 1989; French, 1993b). Attributing the source of an individual's difficulties to their parents, as in Peter's case, has been documented by Galloway et al. (1994: 77), who suggest that the culture of assessment allows professionals to 'explore the deficits in the parenting role' (ibid.). Phillip's teachers seemed to be the most responsive to his transgressions and colluded with him, but this was becoming more difficult as his mobility decreased and they indicated that his desire to retain normality would have to give way to the functionalist imperative to 'accept the help he needs'. The teachers' practices, framed within special needs discourses, constructed individuals as passive objects of their professional knowledge, with impairments and in need of 'fixing' (Ballard, 1996: 38). This was reinforced within the Records of Needs (Chapter 6), in which teachers could report the responsiveness (or submissiveness) of pupils to the support offered.

The pupils with special needs, in contrast, defined themselves as active subjects, with desires rather than needs. Their transgressive actions, whether towards or away from disability, challenged the teachers' notions of support through refusal, avoidance or criticism. The mainstream pupils supported them in this challenge, creating an 'other' of the teachers and voicing empathy but not similarity. Thus, their collusion with the pupils with special needs both included them, in that it promoted a kind of solidarity against the teachers, and excluded them, in generalizing their own dissatisfaction at the 'treatment' of pupils with special needs. There appeared, then, to be three intersecting regimes which were simultaneously including and excluding, and which both constrained and enabled. It is impossible and inappropriate to adjudicate between these: it is tempting to privilege the pupils' desires over the professionally derived needs but celebrating the pupils' transgressions as acts of heroism (Stronach and Maclure, 1997) or demonizing teachers merely establishes teachers and pupils in antagonistic relationships based on resentment of the other. Recognition of the way in which the interactive and competing nature of these regimes is, nevertheless, important in order to increase awareness of the kind of ethical work individuals can do on themselves.

Chapter 6

On the Record

The assessment of children with special needs is fraught with difficulties and its association with resources has made it the source of heated debate (Barton, 1993a; Galloway et al., 1994; Riddell and Brown, 1994). The statement or its Scottish equivalent, the Record of Needs, functions as a legal document of sorts, but there is considerable scope for challenging the recommendations contained therein. Read from a Foucauldian perspective, the statementing or recording process is a disciplinary technique which legitimizes the surveillance and individualization of pupils with special needs and their parents; it also 'engages them in a whole mass of documents that capture and fix them' (Foucault, 1977b: 189). The statementing or recording process can be viewed as operating within a Foucauldian framework of hierarchical surveillance, normalizing judgments and the examination, but these are both contradictory and ambiguous, simultaneously constraining and enabling those who fall under its gaze. The document is treated as if it is an objective and scientific instrument; yet it appears more like a 'pseudo truth regime' (Magill, 1997: 70), which professionals use to record highly subjective and judgmental views about children and their parents. Its gaze appears all encompassing, functioning as if it sees everything; yet it is selective and, as the pupils' accounts suggested in Chapter 5, sometimes misses the point. As a technique of surveillance, the statement or Record of Needs appears remarkably pervasive; but it has been possible for parents to turn the gaze to their advantage and to seek willingly to submit their child and themselves willingly to this kind of scrutiny.

Nine of the eleven pupils who feature in this book had Records of Needs. Phillip, whose muscular dystrophy was progressively limiting his mobility, was in the process of being recorded prior to his transfer to mainstream secondary school. A decision had been taken not to record Fiona, who was hearing impaired, but it was not clear by whom; her parents had certainly not been part of the decision-making process. This chapter examines the way the professionals' gaze operated through the assessment process, looking in particular at the Records of Needs of four pupils (Raschida, Scott, Brian and Peter). In addition, it was possible to observe a meeting to review Peter's Record of Needs, involving various professionals and Peter's mother. These illustrate how far the mechanisms of surveillance reached into the lives of the children and their parents. The chapter begins by exploring the Scottish context in which Records of Needs procedures operate. It then examines the contradictions and ambiguities within the Records of Needs of Raschida, Scott, Brian and Peter and considers more generally how it has constructed both compliant and complicit subjects. The dramatic increase in statementing and recording has led Warnock to label the whole process her 'biggest mistake' (1997: 13). She is objecting, not to problems with the process itself, but with her Committee's failure to realize that individuals would turn the gaze to their own advantage.

Scottish Records of Needs

The Record of Needs, the Scottish version of a statement, was enshrined in the Education (Scotland) Act, 1980 (as amended, 1981). This legislation has two distinctive features. First, unlike its counterpart in England and Wales, it does not make an explicit commitment to integration or inclusion; second, it goes further than the English and Welsh legislation in making provision for parental choice. In these two respects, the Scottish legislation leaves decisions about the placement of children with special needs much more open to parents. Looking at this legislation in the context of children's rights, Clelland and Sutherland (1996) argue that it denies children privacy, since their parents attend all meetings, and accords them a voice only insofar as the local authority considers them fit to express a view. The authors contend that this aspect of the legislation contravenes Article 14 of the United Nations' *Convention of the Rights of the Child* which states that 'all children should have opportunities to express views in processes affecting them' (1989: 191). The Record of Needs is reviewed annually, ensuring a perpetual surveillance of individuals and as Boyne notes, the written record is now 'part and parcel of the operation of power. Individuals are documented, and these writings and files are *for use*' (1990: 114, original emphasis).

The dramatic increase in recording in Scotland — 22.2 per cent over three years from 1993 to 1996, according to the most recent figures available (Scottish Office, 1997) — has presented local authorities with workload difficulties and concerns about demands for resources spiralling out of control. Furthermore, articulate groups of parents representing pupils with dyslexia or Attention Deficit Hyperactivity Disorder have threatened to command disproportionate amounts of local authority budgets (Clark et al., 1997; Riddell et al., 1995). The quest to be defined as 'special' seems to be preoccupying more and more of the population and this blurring of the distinction between normal and special was taken to its extreme by Strathclyde Regional Council's pronouncement that *Every Child is Special* in its 1992 policy document. Jackson was among those who were critical of 'the widening (or dilution) of the definition of special needs to the point where it becomes virtually meaningless . . . For if it is argued that every child is special then there must be a sense in which no child is special' (1993: 12). This was echoed by Galloway et al., who argued that the term special had been misconstrued:

> Warnock extended the term to include the large minority of underachieving and mainly working-class pupils whose education became politically contentious with the economic changes in the late 1970s. Far from being special, there is a powerful argument that the children's needs were absolutely normal, and that the challenge for the school system was, quite simply, to start meeting them. (1994: 14)

Calls for guidance on recording were met in the form of a Government Circular (SOEID, 1996), but which had neither the weight of the Code of Practice (DfE, 1994) issued two years earlier in England and Wales, nor any legal imperative. 'This Circular must not be regarded as giving authoritative legal interpretation of Education or other legislation since that is entirely a matter for the courts' (vii). The aim of the Circular was to 'advise ... and inform' (1996: 1) education authorities and others about the statutory arrangements in Scotland. The document rehearsed the rights of parents and young people with special needs within the 1981 Act and the Children (Scotland) Act 1995 and presented the Record of Needs as a regulatory document:

> The primary objective of recording is to bring more method and stability to the provision of education for children and young persons ... A Record facilitates the identification of the learning difficulties of a child or young person, so that *long-term educational strategies* can be developed especially for him or her. It also enables progress and requirements to be *monitored and reviewed* in a structured way throughout the entirety of a pupil's school career. (SOEID, 1996: 9, original emphasis)

Such an 'overtly regulated approach' (ibid.), the Circular acknowledged, would not be required by everyone. Authorities, therefore, were urged to come up with policies which were 'flexible and able to focus on, and sympathetically reflect, the individual requirements of those for whom they are responsible' (ibid.). In other words, decisions about recording were still to be left to professional discretion, with, of course, the *involvement* of young people and their parents. For those looking for more direction on who should and should not be recorded, this document was disappointing.

The importance of consulting young people about their education was given greater prominence in a discussion paper issued by the government in Scotland:

> The views and aspirations of the individual child or young person with special needs are central to determining provision and meeting their requirements. Their self esteem should be promoted, they should be empowered to participate and encouraged to have high expectations. They must not be regarded as passive recipients of a treatment but active participants in their own learning and development. (The Scottish Office, 1998: 7)

Curiously, only pupils aged 12 or over were 'assumed to be of sufficient age and maturity to form a view', although the document also stated that 'this should not preclude parents, local authorities and other agencies seeking and taking into account the views of younger children' (ibid.).

Education authorities in Scotland, as in other parts of the UK and elsewhere, have struggled to reconcile incompatible policies of integration or inclusion and parental choice alongside the pressure to make cost effective provision. In recent years, councils have attempted to lessen their accountability over the Record of Needs by introducing a greater degree of vagueness and further caveats, a trend which was noted by a Scottish lawyer:

A pernicious practice which has emerged recently in some parts of Scotland is to qualify provisions in Part V of the Record of Needs with phrases such as *according to availability of resources* or *as available*. Such provisions are wholly inappropriate. (Ward, 1990: 154, original emphasis)

The assessment and recording guidelines seemed to offer little advice on how to halt this practice or to specify more clearly who should benefit from recording.

The recording process seeks to regulate and systematize the surveillance and provision of a proportion of the population whose needs are considered significantly greater than the generality of pupils. There have been difficulties, however, in making this distinction and such decisions rest ultimately on their highly subjective judgments. The assessment and recording guidelines point out that identification and assessment 'is not an end in itself' (SOEID, 1996: 10), but a means to making effective provision. The document indicates that an authority could refuse a parental request for the statutory assessment prior to the opening of a Record of Needs if it was considered to be 'unreasonable' (1996: 14). In such a case, however, there is the need for a 'substantive written response' (ibid.), legitimizing the professionals' authority while ensuring they also remain accountable. The guidelines assert that 'the Record of Needs is not a document which should mark out a young child or young person as being different; nor should it be regarded as being a necessary stage in the commitment of resources which would not otherwise be available' (1996: 8).

Clearly the practice of recording pupils has been viewed differently by others, most notably parents. The analysis of the Records of Needs of Raschida, Brian, Scott and Peter suggests that the process simultaneously marks them out as different and seeks to homogenize them.

Techniques of Surveillance

The 'disciplinary gaze' (Foucault, 1977b: 174) is an instrumental kind of surveillance which is insidious and descending, and which captures everyone by making them part of both its operation and its effects. It also has an individualizing effect, marking each person out by his or her distinctive features. Three features of a Foucauldian framework of discipline can be recognized in the process of opening and maintaining a Record of Needs:

- hierarchical observation;
- normalizing judgments;
- the examination.

Recording is used as a scientific and objective technique, based on professionals' expertise, but as a science it appears 'inept, deficient and inconsistent' (Magill, 1997: 69). Its ostensibly omnipresent and omniscient gaze attends selectively to pupils' professionally constructed needs and ignores their desires. It is a disciplinary technique which validates teachers' subjective judgments about pupils and parents, creating compliant subjects, but some discover the value of being looked upon in this way.

Hierarchical Observation

Foucault has noted how hierarchical surveillance ensures a 'hold over the body' (1977b: 177) of individuals with special needs, with a form of power that 'seems all the less *corporal* in that it is more subtly *physical*' (ibid., original emphasis). That is, although it does not have to do violence to or exert pressure upon, the body, its hold on it is much more extensive through its 'uninterrupted play of calculated gazes' (ibid.). The Records of Needs of Raschida, Scott, Brian and Peter provided a framework for hierarchical surveillance, involving professionals and their parents within this hierarchy, parents' knowledge of their child was subjugated by that of professionals. Raschida's report, for instance, detailed the accounts of the various professionals, which read like objective statements of fact. '[Raschida] suffers from retinitis pigmentosa and subsequent restricted visual field, and loss of visual acuity ... visual minimal nystagmus with left divergent squint.' There was, however, some uncertainty as to how far her vision would deteriorate and her consultant ophthalmologist's report contained both confessions to ignorance and guesswork about her future:

> The deterioration is regrettable but not entirely unexpected ... As it gets steadily worse, I imagine her central vision is going to go. We are in a state of ignorance to know whether or not there are any normal activities that make the condition worse. I suspect intuitively that physical activity in the gym is good for the child and should be encouraged.

The 'parental view' was summarized in highly emotive language:

> Parents are now more receptive to the idea that Raschida desperately needs mobility training and Braille to enable her to lead a normal life and seem to be overcoming their initial hesitation about the sort of training for their daughter that they had no hesitation about accepting for their son.

In Scott's Record of Needs, he was described as having been 'diagnosed as suffering from tuberous sclerosis. In his case, his condition is manifested by epilepsy medication'. Scott's Record of Needs, like Raschida's, was dubious about what lay ahead, noting that 'progress for future development is uncertain, though there are grounds for optimism, given progress to date'. Scott's parents were described as having a 'positive attitude': 'Both parents are concerned and caring and wish to do everything they can to assist [his] educational progress ... Both parents are likely to be supportive of school staff in their efforts to teach Scott.' They were praised for presenting 'full and frank' information about Scott's condition and being extremely 'cooperative', but it was also noted that they were 'determined that Scott remains in the normal school system and it is their wish that the Record of Needs be drawn up'.

Brian's Record of Needs began on a very positive note describing him as 'a slow learning child who responds well to a structured learning setting and had consequently developed many of the pre-school skills expected of a child starting school'. His needs were summarized as 'intellectual and social impairment', but his Down's syndrome was mentioned only incidentally, in relation to the two-hour delay in informing his parents of this following his birth. This point is made neutrally within his Record of Needs, yet was part of an 'horrendous' tale told by Brian's mother, suggesting that the gaze had missed the traumatic aspect of this episode. His parents were described in the Record of Needs as '... intelligent caring people who want the best for Brian and have provided a richly stimulating home environment for him. They are anxious to pursue a positive approach which has obviously contributed greatly to Brian's progress.'

Professionals were less positive about Brian's parents in a later review of his Record of Needs in which they were questioning the continuation of his mainstream placement:

> A major problem could be Brian's parents' acceptance of the need for a special school placement. The parental objective at the outset appeared to be for Brian to have the first two years of primary education in mainstream school but the expectation has continued beyond [Primary] 1 and [Primary] 2.

Brian's parents' wish to continue with a mainstream placement was criticized for being unreasonable, and the professionals' aspirations to convince them of 'the need' for segregation suggested that they privileged their own judgment over that of the parents.

Peter's 'case' had been a difficult one for the professionals and it was unusual for a mainstream pupil to have a Record of Needs for emotional or behavioural difficulties. Beyond that it was noted that he had 'no outstanding area of need and requires support across the curriculum'. At a review meeting, the educational psychologist asked Peter's mother to talk about what he was 'like at home' and this was minuted:

> [The psychologist] enquired about Peter's activities at home and had heard that he likes his motor bike, helping on the farm, watching TV, but his concentration often doesn't last long enough for many programmes. Mrs X also mentioned the trouble that Peter gets himself into when he tells lies. She also reported that Peter is worried about his transfer to the Academy.

The professionals took up the issue of Peter's concern about his transfer in the meeting and decided upon an action plan to support this process. The school staff provided reassurance that his skill at sport would help him to be successful, but his peers were critical of his lack of self control in this area. The comments about parents and the ways in which their views were written into the Records of Needs suggests that they were being scrutinized as part of the assessment process rather than active partners, as the rhetoric goes.

Among the professionals dealing with Scott, there appeared to be some contestation within the hierarchy of surveillance, with attempts to privilege certain types of knowledge over others. His Record of Needs contained a copy of a letter his neurologist had sent to the headteacher advising her how to manage his minor fits. '[Teachers] may need to repeat what's been said but [I would] welcome [the] teacher's observation on this. Don't make a fuss. Certainly don't take [the] child out of class and don't call [the] parents.' This letter seemed to privilege medical over educational knowledge and dismissed the parents as either providers or receivers of this knowledge. It was also stated that 'the findings from the psychological assessment confirm [the] views of [his] teachers'. Peter had no medical problems, yet a doctor was required to attend his review meetings as part of the statutory arrangements. At the meeting which was observed, her only comment that 'he has no health problems' was minuted and she made no further contribution to the discussion, appearing to have no mandate to discuss anything outside Peter's health. The professionals working with Brian and Raschida appeared much more united, vowing to 'do everything we can to ensure that her future is less bleak than that forecast'. Creating an 'other' of Raschida's parents seemed to generate an air of professional consensus.

Skrtic (1995) has commented on how the legitimacy of professionals' claims about the validity of their knowledge is premised on positivism and value neutrality. The Records of Needs operated as if the professionals' assessments were precise and scientific, even though these were subjective and uncertain, for example in relation to Raschida and Scott. Parents' contributions were accorded a lower status as 'opinions' or the expression of 'feelings'. The contents of the four pupils' Records of Needs suggest that the professionals' gaze was highly subjective, selective and subjugated parents' views beneath their own 'knowledge tradition' (Skrtic, 1995: 18) and its 'conventional way of structuring the world and seeing its clients' (ibid.). Skrtic argues that it is necessary to 'confront the fact that there is nothing inherently true or correct about [special educational] professional knowledge, practices and discourses' (1995: 20).

Normalizing Judgments

Judgments were made about pupils within their Records of Needs, premised on a binary division of 'normal/abnormal'. Yet, as was suggested in Chapter 5, there seemed to be no absolute notion of the disabled body, with teachers equally critical of pupils for seeking to be either more or less independent. Teachers invoked notions of 'maturity' and 'sensible' behaviour in their judgments about the pupils within an implicit developmental framework. At the same time, however, the pupils were refused aspects of their adolescence, for example, through criticism of the 'vanity' of Raschida or Laura. The normalizing judgments of the teachers were based on a gaze which saw certain things and ignored others. The Record of Needs and Individualized Educational Programmes which were derived from these enabled teachers to both homogenize and individualize pupils.

Raschida was judged as exceeding intellectual norms in relation to her peers, 'at least of average ability' with arithmetic levels which were 'superior to most children of her age'. She matched social norms as a 'socially well adjusted child' who 'relates appropriately with family, peers and adults'. Raschida however, was also judged in terms of her ethnicity, and while it was noted that 'although of bilingual background her English is excellent', her ethnicity was judged to be a major barrier to her success in the eyes of her teachers. Indeed, it was noted that her particular eye condition, retinitis pigmentosa, was a direct result of consanguinity, and this is discussed more fully later in this chapter. Her increasing obstinacy, interpreted in Chapter 4 as transgression, was pathologized within the Record of Needs as part of the normal maturation of a teenager — 'she's at *that* age' (original emphasis). Consideration of a guide dog was, however, sensitive to Raschida's adolescence and to her desires. 'There is the possibility of a guide dog, but Raschida is not keen and there are quite a few disadvantages for teenagers in having a dog of this kind.' Homogeneity and differentiation were combined in the report's recommendations. 'Raschida's educational ability is such that she needs the usual secondary school curriculum. However it needs to be recognised that she has a significant visual difficulty and account [should] be taken of this in the teaching situation.' The report stated that 'mobility training as part of Raschida's social independence is essential', yet as was suggested in Chapter 5, Raschida was also criticized for being so independent that she was unwilling to accept the teachers' support.

In Scott's report, the comparison with the norms of children of the same age was explicit, describing him as 'slightly above norm' in spoken language 'but below age level in most areas'. His response to instruction was recorded as 'poor and inappropriate' and the prognosis for him was negative, since 'even with [his] current skill level he will still be behind many children who will be going on to [secondary school]'. His condition was also judged in relation to medical norms, as 'many children with this condition have other severe and serious symptoms, but [these were] not present in Scott's case'. The reduction in the number of fits he took was explained as 'normal maturation'. The report set out the simultaneously homogenizing and individualizing aims of the professionals:

> Scott requires a normal primary school curriculum, but with allowance and provision made for his areas of specific learning difficulties. [An] individual programme of work should be drawn up with emphasis on (1) extending concentration span and reducing distractibility; (2) perhaps linked with memory training; (3) improving hand/pencil control . . . Scott's individual programme should be followed daily in school and should comprise not less than one hour per school day, though this could be made up by a number of shorter periods. Some one-to-one teaching would be desirable.

Scott was expected to experience both a 'normal' school curriculum and special treatment, aimed at both reducing and highlighting his difference.

Brian's Record of Needs indicated that his 'not always predictable behaviour', in which he 'plays alongside, rather than with other children . . . can sometimes take the form of [that of] a younger child'. There were some good signs that Brian was progressing towards the norm, for example, it was stated that 'Brian's gaining maturity is indicated by the fact that he is moving on to the senior section of the Boys Brigade'. However, it was also made clear that he 'can't be trusted to go to the toilet on his own' as he 'wanders'. His Record of Needs also played out a dispute between professionals and parents regarding his placement in a mainstream school, with both sets of arguments framed within normalizing discourses. His parents, it was noted, 'feel very strongly' that the progress he had 'sustained . . . in all areas of development since his birth' would be best maintained by a mainstream placement. It was also noted that 'local children know him and greet him in the street. All these benefits flow from the fact that Brian attends his local school. [His mother] was therefore very keen for Brian to continue to attend [the primary school]'.

The professionals, however, took a different stance and, in an early review of the Record of Needs (when Brian was aged 8), they drew attention to the increasingly widening gap between Brian and his classmates:

> He has made progress in the past year, but compared with rest of class, Brian is falling further behind. Looking ahead to [Primary] 4, where children are increasingly able to carry out a programme of work and do projects, we can anticipate that the gap between Brian and others will widen. The class teacher will have an increasingly wide range of abilities and needs to cater for.

This had led the professionals to question the validity of his parents' justification for a mainstream placement:

> It is now difficult to sustain the original argument that Brian should have the opportunity to model his educational progress and behavioural patterns on classmates. Educationally he works for most of the day as an individual and his behaviour is not modelled on that of his classmates.

One option suggested by the professionals was placement in a special school. Another consideration, to hold him back for a year, had been discounted on the grounds that his physical maturation was normal, and there would be a 'problem with his size and strength' if he was placed with younger children. The professionals' recommendations for meeting Brian's educational needs favoured greater differentiation through segregation, a strategy which would assist homogeneity by removing him from the mainstream population. This was not stated explicitly, but took the form of an individualized question: 'are we meeting Brian's needs?' and a concern for the demands upon the classroom teacher and the special qualities required to teach Brian: 'not all staff members have the personality/confidence/ability to cope with learning difficulties of this nature'.

In Peter's Record of Needs, his behaviour was attributed partly to immaturity, which affected his social interaction, 'he does not show good judgments when choosing his friends'. It was also described as 'mood related' and although he had made good progress in the classroom, there were 'periods of low spirit'. He was described as 'anxious to be accepted by his peers but lacks maturity and often ends up befriending younger children'. Because of his immaturity, his transfer to secondary was likely to prove stressful and staff sought to increase his participation in mainstream classes 'to provide good role models and prepare for the academy'. The homogenization/individualization duality was evident once more in his Record of Needs, in which Peter was seen as needing to become both more and less dependent on adults:

> [Peter needs] to learn eventually to work and concentrate for longer periods at a time and to be less dependent on teacher supervision, encouragement and direction. The small class numbers and special teaching expertise available in [the special unit] will provide maximum opportunity for Peter to follow appropriate programmes of work at his own pace. The extra adult attention, combined with the individualised work schemes, will give Peter the best possible chance to develop his full potential in all areas.

Exposure to mainstream classes was an important feature of his development, with the emphasis on his presence rather than on sharing the work of his mainstream peers. A normalizing strategy was recommended within mainstream, building on his strengths and ignoring his bad behaviour:

> [The psychologist] made some suggestions, e.g. spellcheck, that might help Peter build on his language strength. He . . . suggested that ignoring poor behaviour and giving responsibility where possible would encourage a better response from Peter rather than a behaviour programme which monitored and recorded bad behaviour.

The results of this approach had been 'good so far' and the psychologist noted that he had been 'encouraged' by the success of this approach.

The Examination

Foucault suggests that the examination holds open a space of domination in which 'disciplinary power manifests its potency' (1977b: 187). Academic, social and emotional aspects of the pupils' lives were scrutinized as part of the recording process and recommendations about 'fixing' observed abnormalities also extended to these areas. Yet the gaze of the professionals was both selective and obtuse.

Raschida was described in her Record of Needs as 'happy enough . . . and socially she is well accepted by her class and gets on well with them but often doesn't make any effort to join in. This is her choice and not the class' fault'. Raschida's emotional response to the deterioration in her vision was recorded. 'After [exams] and loss of vision, Raschida was quite depressed and difficult to motivate. She wanted to leave school, but then wasn't sure. [She] has settled again and will stay for 6th year.' The following year, her report indicated that:

> Raschida had a very successful year academically, but a very difficult and stressful year in terms of deteriorating vision and her attempts to come to terms with this . . . She has had to face the fact that her sight has deteriorated to the point where she had to try to work without being able to see any print or diagrams. For a period of about 3 months, she was very weepy . . . and terribly distressed.

The teachers noted their success in 'talking her through this' and a teacher from the 'Blind School' had given 'invaluable help and insight into the problem and how to deal with adolescents reaching this particular stage'. Raschida had become 'more or less reconciled to the fact of losing her sight'. It was also noted that culturally, Raschida was in a double bind in which her blindness had been caused by consanguinity and this would in turn limit her marriage prospects. A teacher committed her concerns to writing within her Record of Needs file:

> Blind Muslim women are unmarriageable (sic). If anyone did agree to marry her (it would be an arranged marriage from Pakistan) it would only last the minimum time and then the bloke would divorce her *but* would have gained British citizenship. She would then be cast aside; when Muslim women marry, they go to live with the husband's family. If the couple is divorced, the wife is cast out! (original emphasis)

Higher education, rather than marriage, was 'her only way out of this mess' and the staff of the school undertook to ensure that Raschida obtained a university place. The pathologizing of Raschida's adolescence is discussed more fully in Chapter 8.

  Scott's problems with memory and concentration were documented alongside his tendency to be 'wilful and demanding' and the 'determined side to his nature'. He was also considered to be 'easily angered' and was 'obviously a sensitive child', but was 'a pleasant boy'. According to his report, Scott 'mixes well with classmates' and was 'quite happy to be involved in rough and tumble' activities. This sits uneasily alongside his own account of how his mainstream peers called him 'brain dead'. Scott was described as requiring to be both more and less dependent on adults. He was, it said, too inclined to seek help from the learning support teacher, but not willing enough to approach his class teacher. Scott, therefore, needed to become:

> less reliant on parents for support and encouraged, in a gentle but firm way, to approach others, particularly adults (although children in his peer group are also figures with whom he could develop closer links with socially) . . . Scott should be encouraged to ask for help and assistance, particularly in class, and encouraged to approach his class teacher when he faced difficulties in class.

Scott's peer relationships were considered problematic, particularly in view of his impending transfer to secondary school:

Scott has already shown that he is less willing to participate in activities which single him out . . . as children progress to secondary stage, involvement and membership of the peer group becomes more important to them in terms of their self development . . . It became clear that Scott has faced a minor setback over the last 6–8 months. [His] confidence level has dropped and he is less willing to facilitate and initiate contact in the playground or with a wider group of friends, although the main area of weakness is his unwillingness to take the initiative in seeking out help and assistance from the class teacher and peers.

His Record of Needs contained the recommendation that he and his peers should become more mutually dependent:

Another support for Scott would be classmates and perhaps Scott could be made aware that others in class have similar difficulties and that he may be able to help others just as they, in turn, may be able to help him whenever difficulties arise.

These comments on peer relationships have a functionalist orientation and seem to ignore the possibility that the mainstream pupils may not wish to offer help of this kind. Scott and his classmates suggested that their relationships were mediated by much more punitive elements, although the governmental regime of other mainstream pupils had some of the pedagogic features described in Chapter 3.

Brian's unwillingness to cooperate at times both interfered with the assessment process and provided professionals with evidence about his behaviour. It was noted by the speech therapist, for example, that 'it was not possible to assess Brian's verbal comprehension as he was not interested in cooperating fully on this particular occasion'. More generally, Brian was described as 'affectionate and happy', but was considered too dependent on others. His Record of Needs noted a difference of opinion between his parents and professionals over the extent of his ability to interact with his peers:

In class, the extent of natural interactions between Brian and other children in unstructured situations is limited. However [Brian's mother] reported that Brian goes to [junior Boys' Brigade] and Sunday School and doesn't need his parents to be there.

According to his Record of Needs, staff needed to 'draw back to help him become more independent' and within the classroom, Brian required 'support . . . to ensure that Brian understands what is required of him when learning new skills; direction to keep Brian to the task in hand . . . setting of limits on behaviour during playtimes, lunchtimes and enforcing these when necessary.' The support specified here was of a disciplinary kind, aimed at correcting Brian's 'abnormal' behaviour.

Peter's Record of Needs focused mainly on both his emotional and behavioural difficulties and in particular on his 'immaturity'. It indicated that he was 'able to look after his own needs' but detailed his inappropriate friendships and the ways in which his 'concentration can easily be disrupted or [he] can set out to disrupt others. His mood swings affect all work and everyone around.' Association with his mainstream peers was considered likely to reduce his inappropriate behaviour and help in preparation for his transfer to secondary school by providing role models. Staff also planned to familiarize him with the secondary school routines in an effort to reduce the stress they anticipated him experiencing. This seemed to differ from the usual fears of the 'big school' experienced by all pupils, fuelled by rumours of having one's head flushed down the lavatory or receiving birthday beatings. The special needs staff indicated that they would be on hand to support Peter 'if he was unable to cope' in mainstream.

The examination features of the assessment of these four pupils was far reaching, extending into academic, social and emotional areas and, in Raschida's case, included her ethnicity. The process enabled the professionals to specify areas for amelioration and to justify further surveillance, for example, Brian's maturity was to be monitored, while Peter's teachers would observe Peter's ability to 'cope' in the mainstream secondary school. The examination, according to Foucault, is the most important technique of surveillance, holding its subjects in a ritualized gaze:

> In discipline, it is the subjects who have to be seen. Their visibility assures the hold of power that is exercised over them. It is the fact of being constantly seen, of being able always to be seen, that maintains the disciplined individual in his subjection. (Foucault, 1977b: 187)

The gaze of the examination within these four Record of Needs was not only intrusive, extending into social and emotional aspects of the pupils' identity, but was also highly judgmental.

Missing the Point?

The process of recording, 'turning of real lives into writing . . . functions as a procedure of objectification and subjection' (Foucault, 1977b: 192). Hierarchical surveillance legitimized an invasive kind of scrutiny of pupils with special needs and their parents and allowed professionals to privilege their own ostensibly objective judgments over the parents' *feelings*. The normalizing judgments to which pupils with special needs were subjected were simultaneously homogenizing and differentiating. It enabled them to be classified as having a particular *type* of special needs and to find ways of fitting them into the general population, while also maintaining their individuality. Foucault observes that it is easy to understand how this process can be justified within a system of formal equality, since 'within a homogeneity that is the rule, the norm introduces, as a useful imperative and as a result of measurement, all the shading of individual differences' (1977b: 184).

In the dispute between professionals and parents over Brian's placement, both parties supplied normalizing judgments to argue that he should either remain in his mainstream primary or be transferred to a special school. It was evident in his report that within the hierarchy of surveillance, the professionals viewed the parents as intelligent and caring people, but who were nevertheless misguided. The examination features of the recording process were intrusive, particularly in Raschida's case, in which professionals took the liberty of pathologizing her ethnicity along-side her disability and sought to override these in order to ensure a 'less bleak' future for her. The professionals' disciplinary gaze was highly selective and obtuse, missing certain things with its obsessive attention to others. It ignored, for example, the impact of a two-hour delay for Brian's parents before learning that he was disabled and the significance of Raschida's adolescence as anything other than a complicating factor in her adjustment to blindness. It also sought to engineer rela-tionships between Scott and Peter and their mainstream peers, missing the point that Scott's classmates regarded him as 'brain dead', whereas the pupils in Peter's class were critical of his sporting performance, the area which the teachers had assumed he would have credibility. The professionals' gaze also overlooked, or chose to ignore, the pupils' desires.

Pupils with special needs, through the disciplinary techniques of hierarchical observation, normalizing judgments and the examination, become both constructed subjects and objects of power. The Record of Needs provides a juridical space, which appears objective and professional, for making subjective judgments about the pupils and their parents. As far as Raschida, Scott, Brian and Peter were con-cerned, transgressive actions were ignored or criticized, culture was pathologized and a lack of compliance was bemoaned. The document seeks to construct willing and passive subjects within a discourse of needs that simultaneously silences the discourse of desires. It is important to acknowledge, however, that the type of power that attempts to subjectify the pupils is not entirely negative:

> We must cease once and for all to describe the effects of power in negative terms: it *excludes*, it *represses*, it *censors*, it *abstracts*, it *masks*, it *conceals*. In fact, power produces; it produces reality; it produces domains of objects and rituals of truth. The individual and the knowledge that may be gained of him belong to this pro-duction. (Foucault, 1977b: 194, original emphasis)

Thus, it is possible to think of individuals with special needs as *both* passive *and* active, whose subjectivity is constructed for them, and who contribute to that con-struction through compliance *and* resistance (Chapter 4). As Magill points out, individuals may be unable to escape the gaze of power but 'can think about how to turn the gaze to [their] advantage' (1977: 65). Parents appear to have taken up this challenge.

Parents and the Auspicious Gaze?

The process of maintaining and reviewing Records of Needs ensured that indi-vidual pupils were perpetually scrutinized within a hierarchy of professionals for whom surveillance functioned as a 'decisive economic operator, both as an internal part of the production machinery and as a specific mechanism in the disciplinary power' (1977b: 175). Parents, and to a lesser extent pupils, were encouraged to articulate their views, but these were also subjected to scrutiny and used as evid-ence of need in the 'progressive objectification and ever more subtle partitioning of individual behaviour' (1997b: 173). This was particularly evident in relation to Peter and Brian's parents, whose viewpoints were presented as problematic and as possible contributors to their children's special needs.

The parents of the pupils with special needs were part of the objectification and subjection process. Parents' participation in the recording process was closely circumscribed, in terms which marginalized and at times excluded them. Their contribution was portrayed by the professionals as emotional, for example, 'keen', 'feel strongly' or 'strong desire' compared with their own ostensibly more objective knowledge of the pupils' needs. Professionals sometimes sought to protect parents, such as in Scott's case where they were not to be informed of his minor fits during the school day; at other times parents were challenged. This was most evident in relation to Raschida's and Brian's parents, who contradicted what the professionals considered to be in the pupils' best interests. Armstrong argues that the bureaucratization of the assessment procedures may ensure that the main outcome of parental involvement is 'the legitimation of decisions taken by professionals' (1995: 43). The bureaucratization also enables disciplinary techniques of surveillance to function on behalf of parents, at the same time making them objects of that surveillance. The effects of power upon parents are all the more dramatic in that, in seeking to have their child recorded, they are already compliant subjects. They are caught twice in the network of hierarchical observation, as technicians, by observing their own child, and as objects of the descending gaze.

The Record of Needs appears to be a highly effective part of a 'vast, newly articulated set of techniques and tactics that do this work of government and have implications for how we understand ourselves as governed or governors' (Dean, 1996: 209). The pervasiveness of the power, exercised through what Dean calls an 'enfolding of authority' (ibid.), is generated by its apparent legal status. But in practice, the Record of Needs has little weight, as parents who have taken on professionals in an attempt to secure the resources specified in it have discovered. Indeed Brian's parents had not been able to force the local authority to maintain the level of auxiliary provision 'promised' in his Record of Needs and which they understood to be a condition of his remaining in mainstream. However, Susan's mother had taken on the Scottish Office and had secured physiotherapy provision for her (Chapter 5). Barry's mother took a different approach and had put him forward for a television programme in order to raise money for a special bed (Chapter 4). The price of this kind of spectacularization of disability was a high level of visibility, which Barry made clear he hated, while Susan seemed to thrive on it. Peter's mother seemed the most powerless of all the parents, saying when she emerged from a Record of Needs meeting, 'I'm not really sure what was decided.'

The economic climate in which the resources for education provision are restricted appears to have reversed concerns about labelling or stigma associated with being identified as having special needs. A Record of Needs has become a valued commodity which is viewed, misguidedly or otherwise, as opening the door to additional resources. The cut-off point, where a child is or is not deemed to require a Record of Needs is in no sense clearly defined and children who are not recorded are thought by parents or professionals to be disadvantaged by not having a label which distinguishes them clearly from other pupils. Disputes about who should and should not be recorded are also about candidacy for disciplinary power; it is perhaps surprising that parents are often the most vociferous in demanding to have their child recorded, since this also requires being subjected to extensive surveillance. Foucault reminds us that where there is power, there is also the capacity for resistance (1997b). In a climate of resource constraints, however, distance from the norm has become valued and the Record of Needs has become a form of power which is coveted rather than resisted.

Warnock's Regrets

The dramatic increase in requests to have children statemented or recorded and the bitter disputes which have ensued, particularly in England and Wales, has led Baroness Warnock to regret the whole idea:

> Unless someone is brave enough to bring to an end what I regard as our — my — greatest mistake, namely statementing, money will still be squandered in the same way it is now . . . the problems to do with statementing are almost insoluble and very expensive. The only way to solve it is to cut through the whole thing. (1997: 13)

She went on to suggest that the situation had forced authorities and individual teachers into dishonest tactics:

> The horror of the situation is the confrontations arising over provision . . . local authorities are forbidding teachers to appear at the tribunals because they are afraid it would mean more money being spent. Although teachers can be summoned to appear before a tribunal, you are not going to get them to give really truthful testimony in that sort of circumstance — when they have a gun at their back from the local authority. Being summoned does not prevent them from lying if the authority has so instructed them. It is a terrible situation to be in. (1997: 13)

Although the situation in Scotland is not marked by the same degree of contestation as in England and Wales, considerable concern has been voiced about the demand for Records of Needs. Warnock regrets the idea of statementing and, by implication recording, not because it has failed to serve the interests of pupils and parents or has become too invasive. Rather, she has come to lament the ways in which parents and others have recognised that its gaze is an auspicious one and have turned it to their advantage.

Chapter 7

Between Two Worlds

Fiona (15) lived in the space between two worlds of the deaf and the hearing. She was partially deaf and attended her local mainstream secondary school. Her teachers described her as 'hearing impaired', but she and her mainstream peers preferred the term 'deaf'. At home, she was deaf, like her brother, mother and grandmother, but her sister and father both had normal hearing. She had exposure, then, to both deaf and hearing worlds, but from her account seemed to be fully part of neither. This is a case study of splitting. Deaf people have their own values, history and, above all, a sense of community (Morris, 1991; Taylor and Bishop, 1991), but Fiona appeared not to see herself as fully part of that community, even though her deafness featured in her account of herself. Fiona's experience of mainstreaming was excluding and marginalizing, by dissolving difference (Kyle, 1993), transforming her deafness into a disability and 'denying the existence of an *alien* Deaf culture' (Corker, 1996a: 51, original emphasis). Booth (1988) contends that the silencing of deaf culture within mainstream schools amounts to an extreme prejudice and her transgressive practices could be interpreted as a 'survival tactic unknowingly cultivated by those caught between' two worlds (Hartsock, 1996: 49). Wynter has suggested, however, that the status of liminality experienced by individuals forced to live out two realities gives them a 'cognitive edge' over others (1987: 235). This chapter focuses on Fiona, the governmental regime of her mainstream peers, her transgression out of deafness, and the teachers' practices. It explores similar themes to those contained earlier in the book, but Fiona's experience of liminality from both the hearing and deaf worlds seemed to merit consideration in a separate chapter. The unique features of deaf culture and identity are also considered and the chapter ends with a discussion of the collective transgression of deaf people, who have demanded 'recognition as a cultural and linguistic minority group' (Gregory, 1993: 5).

Introducing Fiona

> I'm tall, with brown hair and I'm deaf. My mum and brother's deaf and so's my gran and I have a deaf cousin . . . I'm mad about horses and I'm quite funny and always happy. (Fiona)

Fiona said she had learned some sign language, but had little use for it. She only knew two people of her own age who were deaf and signed with neither them nor the deaf members of her family. Sometimes, however, her classmates asked her to show them how to say something in sign language, giving it a slightly exotic quality rather than as an important element of communication between them. Fiona described a kind of a hierarchy of deafness within her home. Her mother, who was profoundly deaf, could not answer the telephone. This job was normally given to her father or sister, the hearing members of the family, or to Fiona's brother, who had a phonic connection to use with the telephone. Fiona said she used to answer the telephone and could hear providing the person on the line spoke loudly and clearly and the television volume was turned down. On one occasion, however, she was unable to make any sense of the person speaking and she had never answered it since then, because she hated situations in which she 'looked stupid'. Fiona said she had never gone to the local deaf club since people signed there and she felt she would not 'fit in'. She said she was more comfortable with her hearing friends at school, but found some difficulties in fitting in there also, because of her deafness.

Fiona's Mainstream Peers and Governmentality

In Chapter 3, it was argued that the mainstream peers of pupils with special needs played an important role as gatekeepers of inclusion. Their regime of governmentality, with its pastoral power, pedagogic, transgressive and punitive features, could, it was suggested, support or restrict the participation of pupils within mainstream. Fiona's peers were equally influential, yet their governmentality was highly ambivalent, since it both supported her inclusion in mainstream and erased aspects of her deaf identity. The mainstream pupils colluded with her to help improve her performance within a hearing environment, but also provided coercive markers of disability by inadvertently making communication difficult. Fiona described how her peers often forgot about her deafness in conversations with her:

> Sometimes in school I can't hear what people say behind my back or if they don't turn their face to me or they speak too fast or when people cover their faces with their hands or I have to keep asking what people said. It's embarrassing and sometimes I don't ask then I don't know what to do.

She said her friends understood what it was like to be deaf and they helped her by 'not mumbling'. However, they often 'forgot' to speak clearly, which she both welcomed, because it suggested they were inattentive to her difference, and found difficult, because it excluded her. Fiona indicated that she was happy at school but that this had not always been the case. At primary school she had been called names by other pupils. While she was still at primary, she was aware that her older brother (also deaf) was being bullied at secondary school and so was afraid to make the transfer. However, her parents visited senior staff at the school and Fiona experienced no bullying when she moved there. Despite this, she remained nervous about her hearing aid becoming a coercive marker of disability in secondary, as it had been in primary:

> When I came to the academy I was afraid and worried because I thought nobody would like me because I am deaf. At my old school boys called me 'deafie' and 'phonic ear'. I sometimes get angry and upset and sometimes tell the teacher and the teacher will tell the person to get a row. I thought that the boys from my last school would call me names.

Fiona had not experienced any name-calling, but nevertheless said she was 'wary' of some of the boys in the school.

The governmentality of Fiona's peers was mainly pedagogic and collusive, involving specific efforts to correct her linguistic errors. Their help with pronunciation of new or difficult words seemed to be aimed at supporting her assimilation into their hearing culture. At the same time, however, they were concerned about how she might interpret such help, revealing an element of pastoral power. 'Sometimes if she can't pronounce words, we just tell her what it is, like the other day she couldn't say "brochure" and I just said it was "brochure" and then she kept saying it right . . . We try not to make her feel bad if she's not hearing right.'

The mainstream pupils' conduct seemed to be mediated by the kind of proactive and individualizing guesswork practised by Raschida and Laura's peers. Thus, they sought to help her out, but tried to anticipate her likely response to this and adjusted what they said accordingly. By telling Fiona how to pronounce a word, they were acting conspiratorially, giving her factual information to assist her linguistic competence, but they tried to ensure that they did not highlight her difference in the process. They seemed to help Fiona's mainstream performance by disclosing some of the rules of language. Their relationship did not appear relaxed, with the kind of quickfire interchange which Kyle (1993) describes; nor was it particularly tense, despite the difficulties Fiona sometimes experienced. Rather, it seemed to be functional, in which the mainstream pupils colluded to help her perform as effectively as possible within the mainstream environment.

The accounts of Fiona's peers also oscillated between similarity and difference. They described her as 'deaf, but she can hear things OK' and drew attention to her obsession with horses, comparing her with another 'horse mad' classmate. They said that being in a secondary school was better than going to a special school for deaf pupils because she could be 'treated normally'. This was important because 'there's nothing wrong with her, apart from her deafness'. They saw her as more like them than like other deaf people. 'Well she knows a couple of people who are deaf, but she's just like us really, just that she's deaf.'

The mainstream pupils' accounts, although positive about Fiona and her inclusion in mainstream, were also assimilationist, erasing Fiona's deafness from her identity. As the only mark of her 'difference' from them, they sought to remove it by constraining, through helping, her to behave like a hearing person. There was no indication in the pupils' accounts that they recognized positive features of deaf culture and language, although they had enjoyed learning a few phrases in sign language. The operation of their regime of governmentality required them to be alert to language difficulties experienced by Fiona and to try to give her help unobtrusively. Fiona's mainstream peers' regime seemed to work only on their own conduct and they did not monitor other pupils' behaviour towards Fiona, as did the peers of Sarah, Brian or Peter (Chapter 3). Yet they seemed to regard conduct towards her as unproblematic and uncontroversial.

In one sense, the governmentality of Fiona's peers assisted her inclusion, by ignoring her deafness and helping her to learn the rules of a successful mainstream performance. In another sense, the mainstream pupils' regime could also be considered punitive by sometimes making it difficult to follow their conversation and because, like her teachers, they forced Fiona to transgress out of her deafness.

Fiona's Transgressive Practices

Fiona's transgression sought to move away from her deafness and involved pretending to hear and attempting to keep up with the verbal interactions of her peers. This was not always successful. When Fiona's friends 'forgot' about her deafness and made communication difficult, by mumbling or facing away from them; rather than remind them that she was deaf, she pretended she understood them, practising a kind of rehearsed carelessness by nodding (Garfinkel, 1967: 172). She sometimes felt she had lost the thread of a conversation and to keep interrupting, by 'saying pardon' would be 'annoying for everybody else'. So she frequently just nodded, which sufficed until she was asked a question, to which she usually replied 'I'm not sure'. This kind of neutral answer allowed the conversation to carry on offering more clues as to its content. Fiona seemed to be transgressing out of a deaf identity which, she said, worked most of the time, since people forgot she was deaf. When it didn't, she was left indecisive about whether to own up and ask for something to be repeated or to continue feigning understanding. She did not work on her peers' regime in the way that Raschida and Laura did and her successful transgression out of deafness contributed to the denial of her deaf identity, by encouraging further forgetfulness among her peers.

Fiona's hearing aid provided a coercive marker of disability which she sought to avoid. In a story which had parallels with Raschida's account of 'losing' her cane in the lake, Fiona indicated that her hearing aid was broken and it had been 'away for ages getting fixed'. This suited her because she 'hated it':

> I have to wear a hearing aid and so does my mum, my granny and my two great aunties and my cousin . . . My brother used to wear one. I'm used to it because I [have] had a hearing aid for 11 years. But sometimes I don't understand the words and I hate my phonic ear.

Not having her hearing aid helped Fiona in her attempt to 'fit in' among her peers, as it represented a coercive marker of disability, but it was also difficult to function without it and Fiona spoke of how the secondary school was a difficult environment. 'When people speak to me there is a lot of noise. I can't hear what they are saying because in the academy there are 1200 people in school who make such a noise that I can't hear.'

Ladd presents an image of the social encounters of a deaf person in mainstream:

> Meanwhile he misses the crux of just about everything; jokes, quick remarks, frantically flipping his head from one face to another like a Wimbledon umpire, trying to catch the last bit of whoever was talking and trying to piece together what so and so did, what so and so meant . . . He begins to build up an image of himself as a stumbling, blundering retard, breaking off his sentences half way through because he is sure no one wants to hear what he wants to say, lumbering around hopelessly on the fringe of things. After a while, the initial goodwill extended to him by his school mates dries up. The truce is over and battle begins; he becomes one of the butts of all the digs and jokes. (1991: 91–2)

Fiona did not appear to be battling with her peers, nor was she the butt of their jokes. Nevertheless, access to the basic quickfire interchange (Kyle, 1993), so important to adolescents, was often denied to her, placing her both inside and outside the hearing world. Her transgression involved keeping up with conversations and feigning understanding when she lost track, creating an otherness which seemed to lack the playfulness which Foucault portrayed as a 'form of combat with pleasures to be mastered' (Simons, 1995: 73). It was characterized instead by tension and fear of discovery. Such transgressive practices might have been unnecessary had her deaf identity been valued within the school. On the other hand, it is important not to regard such transgressive practices as having any less value than those practised by the other pupils who feature in this research. Indeed, writers exploring the experience of living in two ethnic realities have suggested that those who are forced to 'exist in the interface' (Hartsock, 1996: 49) learn to see deep structural meanings in surfaces, which gives them an advantage over 'the disembodied and singular subject of Western thought' (ibid.). Anzaldúa (1987) suggests that all marginalized individuals forced to live with two partial identities acquire this ability to look beneath the surface and Wynter (1987) argues that this allows individuals to make 'potentially innovative contributions' (cited in Hartsock, 1996: 49).

Mainstreaming and the Silencing of Deaf Culture

Fiona's experiences of mainstreaming were complex and contradictory. Her transgressive practices, in which she pretended to hear normally, frustrated her teachers and their attempts to support her. Their support, framed within a discourse of needs, problematized Fiona's deafness as a disability and was dependent on her accepting the limitations imposed by this. Her teachers encouraged assimilation into a hearing environment and eroded her deaf identity and culture, while also constraining her to be disabled through her daily sessions with a peripatetic teacher of the hearing impaired. This took the place of French, a subject which it was assumed would be of no value to her because she was deaf, even though as Booth and Ainscow (1998a) note, foreign languages can be taught successfully to deaf pupils.

Fiona's teachers attempted to discourage her transgressive attempts to pretend to hear and understand things which she clearly had not. One teacher spoke of her efforts to make Fiona seek help. 'Through the support from [the learning support teacher] and the teacher of the hearing impaired we try to make her responsible for saying what she doesn't understand.' Fiona's English teacher made a similar comment about her reluctance to seek help, but also wondered about the extent of her deafness.

> She needs to sit at the front if we are talking. In group discussion work I'm not always sure that she is fully involved. She will sit back and let everybody else put their bit in and has to be encouraged to have her say. Possibly she is not hearing as well as she could be doing.

Her computing teacher said he was unsure whether her unwillingness to 'speak up' was connected to deafness or shyness. 'I discovered also [that] she seems to be able to, when she does look at you, to lip read a bit. She has never had to say or ask me to repeat something that I have said to her. Whether that is shyness on her part I don't know but she might have understood it.' Fiona's reticence with this teacher could well be attributable to shyness or, perhaps more likely, a reaction to his crass attempts at communication, which provided a coercive marker of disability:

> Sometimes I would speak to her but the difficulty of that is, typically, you are used to talking over somebody's shoulder and so if she is not looking at me then I would develop, not sign language, [but] it would be to point to the screen and signal and she would understand to do what I was pointing to and I would use sort of mannerisms like ones and twos with my fingers.

Fiona's teachers, speaking within a discourse of needs, said that admitting that she could not hear or understand particular things was a necessary part of 'coming to terms' with her disability and easing her into the world of work. The learning support teacher reported improvements in Fiona's 'willingness' to ask for help:

> She will say that 'we have to do this' or 'I don't understand'. She didn't always do that but she is getting a lot better at that, so we are really trying to put the responsibility back to her and again I go back to our original thinking that making a good citizen, we want to get it into her that if she doesn't understand something she must say so and if you can do that in the world of work then you stand a better job of being a good worker and keeping your job than if you just sit quietly and do nothing . . . I think you have to be able to admit that you can't do something in order to ask for help so if we can do that in a way that she finds comfortable then hopefully we will be able to transfer to a situation where she is not so comfortable and that is what we are trying to do.

An earlier report had suggested that Fiona was manipulative, trying to get her own way by claiming to be unable to do something. She needed 'firm handling, to which she will respond'. Fiona's learning support teacher sent a memo to the mainstream staff instructing them to override her pretence that she could hear, by checking constantly that she understood their instructions:

> Please ensure she understands by asking her to repeat [instructions]. Remember if you ask 'Do you understand?' Fiona will say yes whether she does or not. Speaking slowly will increase understanding as Fiona can lip-read to a certain degree.

The memo also referred to her unwillingness to wear her hearing aid and asked teachers to check that Fiona was wearing it and that it was switched on. Fiona's English teacher said that she was regularly without it. 'It helps if Fiona has her phonic ear but she quite often has it broken or damaged or it is not working for various reasons. She hasn't had it for quite some time now. If she has that I feel more confident that she is hearing what I am saying.' Her computing teacher also spoke about it being broken, but also expressed relief, since the computers interfered with it anyway:

> I discovered when I spoke to the class at the start of the lesson and she had her hearing aid on and she was picking up all the background high pitched noises and so on that I think the monitors produce . . . The computer, though, may be partially to blame because I believe they do put out a radio frequency. As her gadget is operated by a radio technology, it is possibly picking the sound up from that. About that time I think it broke down so she had to send it away.

Fiona expressed an alternative view that her communication difficulties were caused by teachers who 'speak too fast'.

Fiona was visited daily by a specialist teacher of the hearing impaired, while her mainstream peers went to French. In some ways, the teacher provided a bridge between the hearing and the deaf world; she also limited the connection with other deaf people by constructing Fiona's deafness as a disability and focusing on Fiona's (in)ability to function in a hearing environment. This particular teacher had accompanied Fiona throughout most of her primary career and followed her when she moved to secondary. The purpose of the teacher's visits was to try to help Fiona overcome some of the language problems which came (inevitably) from being born deaf. Part of this involved explaining the common words and phrases which had confused her when she had interpreted them literally, for example 'head in the clouds' or 'a sweet tooth'. They spent one hour each day going through these, introducing new words, catching up on homework or simply talking. Their conversations often focused on Fiona's experience of deafness and her feelings generally about herself. Fiona said she valued these conversations and thought the teacher was 'really nice'. The specialist teacher commended Fiona's class teachers' positive attitude towards her, which had in turn encouraged her to seek help. 'I have great admiration for the way the staff at [the academy] have made it possible for Fiona to relax and feel able to ask for help.' She also gave testimony to Fiona's fighting spirit and tenacity, which she considered to be both an asset and a flaw:

She gets little encouragement from home and is always told how hopeless she is. [She] can definitely have a mind of her own and won't be moved once she's decided something . . . [She] can become easily discouraged . . . She needs a great deal of patience and support.

The specialist teacher's comments emphasized the importance of Fiona accepting the limitations imposed by her deafness. During her time with Fiona, the teacher said she had watched her growth with satisfaction. 'I have worked with her for more than six years and have never seen her as happy, relaxed and confident as she is at present.'

The mainstream pupils seemed aware, but uncritical, of their teachers' classroom practices. 'The teachers speak louder and make sure they're facing her when they're speaking to the class and make sure her hearing aid's on . . . They make sure she's sitting at the front of the class.' Actions by the teachers, which appeared as coercive markers of disability to Fiona, seemed unremarkable to Fiona's peers, in contrast with how Raschida and Laura's peers viewed them. Fiona's teachers helped her to adapt to the hearing environment of the mainstream school, but also undermined her transgressions by constructing her deafness as a disability.

There were no opportunities for Fiona to learn sign language within the school, even though this might have assisted her language development more generally. Hoffmeister argues that this constitutes 'proof of an establishment that creates rules under the colonial framework of audism' (1996: 187–8). The support offered by Fiona's specialist teacher of the hearing impaired helped her to function in the hearing world. Yet her tendency to view Fiona's deafness as a disability, rather than as a distinctive language and identity, acted as a coercive marker of disability. It has been argued that deaf people should not be denied access to deaf culture (Kyle, 1993; Ladd, 1991; Lane, 1995) and sign language is an intrinsic part of this:

The sensory world is a very different world without audition and sign language is possibly the only way of fully expressing the meaning that this world has, for it is a gestural–visual–spatial language. (Corker, 1993: 150)

Ladd (1991) argues that the denial of access to sign language is part of the oppression experienced by deaf people:

How sickening, I thought. I had always been taught that lip-reading and hearing aids were adequate, yet only now could I realise that they were, at best, crutches. They were not legs. It became clear that my legs were in fact sign language. It seemed as if I had spent all of my time on crutches, when I could have had legs. (Ladd, 1991: 96)

Inclusion for Fiona implied assimilation and a denial of her deaf identity (Corker, 1993), forcing her to be less deaf and more disabled. Partial exclusion, in the form of daily withdrawal helped her acquire the language which was lost through deafness, but also disabled her, by othering her deafness as a problem to be overcome, rather than as a language and culture of its own. Inclusion which assimilates deaf culture and creates abnormality out of deafness (Booth, 1988) has the potential to be 'the most dangerous move yet against the early development of a deaf person's character, self-confidence and basic sense of identity' (Ladd, 1991: 88). The inclusion of deaf pupils in mainstream schools has been questioned because of the way teachers have constructed deafness as a disability and exposed children to experience a 'totally exclusionary program called inclusion' (Lane, 1995: 182).

Making a Disability out of Deafness

The greatest difficulty experienced by deaf individuals seems to be a pathologizing of their deafness, focusing on their inability to function in a hearing world and using the language of infirmity (Hoffmeister, 1996). Special education departments in schools and other institutions represent 'discursive straightjackets that confine Deaf culture to pathological constructions' (Dirksen, Bauman and Drake, 1997: 307). Sign language is portrayed, not as a minority language, but as a 'system of communication' (Hoffmeister, 1996: 184). This kind of medicalization is, of course, an experience which is shared by other disabled people (Fulcher, 1989; Oliver, 1996). Yet it has been suggested that the consequences for deaf people are more significant, since it simultaneously negates deaf culture and damages identity, by creating individuals who are 'caught between two or more worlds because they struggle for an identity which reflects accurately who they are' (Corker, 1996b: 56).

Deaf people, Corker suggests, may behave like chameleons, which change colour to hide from predators, becoming more or less deaf according to whom they are with. This is likely to create enormous tensions among individuals and a sense of 'shameful difference' (Goffman, 1963: 156) in which individuals struggle to gain acceptance in both worlds. '. . . individuals with a stigma . . . may have to learn about the structure of interaction in order to learn about the lines along which they may reconstitute their conduct if they are to minimize the obtrusiveness of their stigma' (Goffman, 1963: 127).

Corker stresses the importance of deaf people 'gaining recognition, acceptance and affirmation of deafness, without assumptions about *deaf identity* as the driving force in their lives' (1996b: 61, original emphasis). This involves simultaneously foregrounding and backgrounding individuals' deafness and although it involves being essentialist, it is important to recognize those features which contribute to the unique experience of deaf individuals. Wright, for example, points to:

> an undramatic but not minor disadvantage of deafness, felt less positively by the deaf than their hearing friends: having to dispense with the easy exchange of trivialities that is oil to the wheels of conversation and to the business of living. The use of language as gesture, as reassuring noise rather than an instrument of specific communication, is largely denied the deaf. (1993: 6–7)

Wright also refers to the effect of being born into a world with no communication as 'like watching a silent film without captions' (1993: 236). Kyle argues that deafness is a complex essence which interferes with communication but does not prohibit it:

> Deafness strikes at the very heart of the educational endeavour as it means that information cannot be gained reliably and effectively through speech and hearing. Yet it is not a disability which takes away language — deaf people have a different language to use. (1993: 217)

As the Labour MP Jack Ashley, who gradually became deaf, testifies, however, this interference is far reaching and can render one socially incompetent:

> I had not expected to understand much but the reality was a chilling experience. I understood very little of what was said and, to add to my discomfort, I had no idea where to look. By the time I swivelled round to locate a speaker he would be half way through his question; a brief one would be finished before I could start to make any sense of it. This did not seem like the Chamber where I had vigorously interrupted other speakers and impatiently waited my turn to speak. It was transformed into a mysterious, menacing arena where I could be trapped into misunderstanding the arguments and passions which swiftly ebbed and flowed. It would be all too easy to make a fool of myself: somehow I had to make sense out of this silence and as I sat there I reflected on the daunting prospect. (1991: 215)

Essentializing deafness inevitably highlights its negative impact on so-called normal interaction. It also provides scope, however, for recognizing and celebrating the positive features of deafness. The final section of this chapter explores the collective transgression among deaf people who have expressed pride in their identity and demanded respect for their culture and language.

'We are deaf not disabled': Collective Transgression

Fiona's attempts at transgressing out of her deafness arose, it is suggested, from a failure within her mainstream school to recognize and value deafness as a culture and language. Her transgressions were often only partially successful as performances and even her successes created further difficulties by encouraging her peers to forget about the need to communicate clearly. The deaf community, in contrast, have transgressed *into* their deaf identity and have demanded greater recognition as a 'separate linguistic cultural group' rather than as disabled people (Corker, 1993).

Hoffmeister suggests that deaf people have been 'forced to do battle' (1996: 174) whilst Gearheart, Mullen and Gearheart contend that the deaf community is unique in responding so vociferously and effectively. 'The phenomenon of a group of exceptional individuals organizing and speaking up on their own behalf is perhaps unique to this population' (1993: 262). Corker (1996b) warns that the deaf community does not present a united front and can itself be oppressive, with membership depending on individuals' demonstration of group loyalty. Yet it has occasionally reached new heights of 'oppositional consciousness', for example, during the protest by deaf students (Christiansen and Barnett, 1995) at Gallaudet University in 1988. As well as achieving the goal of ensuring that the new president was deaf, the participants also acquired 'an enhanced pride in being deaf and in being part of a vibrant community with a unique language and culture' (1995: xxi). The transgressive actions of the deaf community have been antagonistic, fighting oppression and demanding recognition of deaf culture and language and their collective identity has arguably made them more powerful than individuals practising transgression on their own. However, Sacks notes that deaf people in the United Kingdom still experience discrimination in education and employment and 'painful social isolation' (1990: 164).

Deaf children have been part of an acrimonious battle over how they should be taught: on one side have been proponents of oral methods, which equate with assimilation discourses; on the other side have been those who see sign language as a means of preserving the culture and identity of deaf people. Sacks traces the contest between signing and oral methods back to 1776, when France's de l'Epée, a protagonist of signing, challenged oralists such as Pereire and Deschamps. Signing gained widespread acceptability, heralding a 'great impetus of deaf education and liberation' (1990: 24) until a century later when this approach became questioned on the grounds of its interference with speech. The American Gallaudet saw advantages in both approaches, but encountered staunch reformers, particularly among the oralists, including Alexander Graham Bell. Signing was officially proscribed in 1880, following the Congress of Educators of the deaf in Milan, which curiously denied teachers of deaf children a vote. This led, observes Sacks, to a century of failure, and it was only in the 1960s that serious questions were asked about the damage caused by a reliance on oralist methods. Teachers of deaf children continue to be a powerful force within education today.

The failure of the pupils and teachers in Fiona's school to recognize and value her deafness as a language and culture can be read as an act of oppression (Booth, 1988). Had there been more explicit attempts to acknowledge and value the cultural distinctiveness of deafness, Fiona might not have felt 'undoubtedly motivated by a desire to conceal' (Lynas, 1986b: 180). She might also have avoided 'struggling to understand' and feeling 'angry and upset' when she could not. Fiona sought to transgress out of her deafness because of its negative connotations within the mainstream school and the way in which it had been constructed as a disability, forcing her to 'co-operate in promoting a view . . . of herself as disabled' (Lane, 1995: 177). The transgressive practices of the pupils who feature elsewhere in this book have been valorized as acts of creativity. Fiona's transgression can be read in a similar vein and as giving her an advantage over her peers by putting at her disposal different ways of knowing. Yet, it can also be considered to be a far less positive kind of transgression than the collective response of the deaf community, which has declared: 'We are proud of our language, culture and heritage. Disabled we are not!' (Bienvenu, 1989: 13).

Chapter 8

Gender and Sexuality

The silencing of the gender and sexuality of disabled people (Barron, 1997; Shakespeare, Gillespie-Sells and Davies, 1996) is a form of oppression which makes them feel that disability is a breed of its own, neither masculine nor feminine (Shakespeare et al., 1996). The normative gaze (Young, 1990a) makes an aesthetic judgment about disabled bodies which may exclude individuals from personal relationships by pronouncing them unattractive or simply refuses to see gender and sexuality in disabled people. Although disabled writers have argued whether the silencing of gender and sexuality is worse for men or women, all have agreed that 'the assumption of asexuality is a contributing factor towards the disregard of disabled people' (Shakespeare et al., 1996: 10). Lonsdale has highlighted a tendency towards 'treating women in general as sexual playthings and yet women with disabilities as asexual' (1990: 7), contributing to a double bind in which 'women with disabilities are made to feel failures if they don't succeed and larger than life if they do' (1990: 67). Thomson suggests that the disabled woman occupies an 'intragender position' (1997: 288), defined against both the masculine figure and the normative woman, whereas Murphy portrays his own progressive disablement and that of other males as 'symbolic castration in impotence' (1990: 96), a perception arising from the expectation of male competence. This is exacerbated by the public perception of disabled people as 'either libidinous dwarfs, or, more commonly, completely asexual' (1990: 97). In recent years a number of disabled people have analysed this silencing or attribution of asexuality as part of the oppression they experience and called for their rights as sexual people to be acknowledged alongside other basic human rights. Yet even the disability movement has been criticized for ignoring the concerns of disabled women, especially regarding sexuality, reproduction and mothering (Kallianes and Rubenfield, 1997) and gay and lesbian individuals have reported oppression and isolation from within the disabled community (Appleby, 1994; Shakespeare et al., 1996).

The young people in this research experienced considerable silencing of their gender and sexuality by their mainstream peers, teachers and parents, which extended beyond the usual sanitizing and asexual practices of schooling (Singh, 1995; Walkerdine, 1990). The mainstream pupils, within their regime of governmentality, either ignored or deliberately erased their gendered and sexual identities. In Brian's case, however, there was scope within the mainstream pupils' governmental regime for breaking some of the usual rules of sexual contact. Teachers silenced gender and sexuality within their discourse of needs whereas parents did this by their apparent reluctance to look beyond the pupils' school lives and to consider matters of relationships and parenthood. Nevertheless the pupils' transgressive practices were at times directed against these silences and erasures, seeking to assert themselves as gendered and sexual subjects. The pupils' transgressive practices enabled them to challenge the obligations on them to be simultaneously disabled and 'exempted from the *male* productive role and the *female* nurturing one' (Asch and Fine, 1997: 241, original emphasis). This chapter explores the ways in which mainstream pupils, teachers and parents silenced gender and sexuality among the pupils with special needs and considers the pupils' attempts to insert gender and sexuality into their identities and experiences. In the final part of the chapter, the resistance within the disability movement to the silencing of gender and sexuality is explored.

Mainstream Pupils' Disqualifiers

Within the mainstream pupils' regime of governmentality, the gender and sexuality of pupils with special needs tended either to be treated with disinterest or deliberately erased. The mainstream pupils' pastoral power allowed them to show concern for the welfare of pupils with special needs in ways which disqualified them as individuals with a gender or sexuality. Furthermore, their pedagogic strategies assumed a greater maturity for themselves and infantilized pupils with special needs, particularly those with moderate learning difficulties. Brian and Graham's peers, for example, talked of how they acted as disciplinarians or role models 'for their own good' and 'to help them get better'. Progress was judged in terms of maturation, and Graham's peers observed that he had matured considerably since coming into their class. One of Barry's peers suggested that his asexuality was one of his most attractive features. 'He's nice. He's easy to talk to. He's easier to talk to because he doesn't make assumptions . . . I've told him things that I wouldn't tell my best friend, for example, because he's easier to talk to.' She hinted at a kind of impotence on Barry's part that made any 'secrets' she told him safe and any feelings she expressed unlikely to be interpreted as an overture towards him. Susan's peers praised her dependence on them, in a way that could have been seen as engendering her in terms of femininity and passivity (Shildrick and Price, 1996). Occasionally other pupils were acknowledged as gendered subjects. Phillip's peers, for example, mentioned that he 'liked some of the girls'. It was suggested in Chapter 3 that Brian, who had Down's Syndrome, was allowed to cross boundaries of personal contact with boys and girls which were closed to others. However, this appeared to be neutralized by the pastoral and pedagogic features of the pupils' governmental regime.

The punitive aspects of the mainstream pupils' governmental regime excluded pupils in fairly brutal ways, for example the description of Scott as 'brain dead' or the bullying of Sarah. The more subtle isolation of Graham, on account of his obsession with football, was perhaps even more unfortunate, since he had somehow managed to misjudge a central part of Scottish male culture. Each of these exclusionary processes seemed also to disqualify the pupils as gendered or sexual subjects by giving them a kind of 'rolelessness or social invisibility' (Thomson,

1997: 285). Sarah's peers, however, in acknowledging the impact of the bullying on her, recognized how her future relationships would be damaged by a loss of confidence.

Teachers and Parents: Neutralizing Maturity

Chapter 5 explored how the teachers' professional practices, based on a discourse of needs, often challenged the pupils' transgressive practices. The teachers also silenced the gender and sexuality of the pupils, either by ignoring these aspects or by pathologizing adolescence as a difficult stage which interfered with their attempts to provide support. Parents seemed reluctant to story gender and sexuality into their children's futures and so presented partial conjecture about what lay ahead.

Teachers and Their Discourse of Needs

Most of the teachers' concerns about the pupils related to support and in Chapter 5, it was suggested that these often clashed with the pupils' desires. In many cases, the teachers saw the pupils' unwillingness to accept support as limiting their achievements. Thus, criticisms of Susan's reluctance to do things for herself, Raschida's failure to acknowledge the extent of her blindness and Peter's claims that he was a 'spastic' were justified on the grounds that they would restrict their futures. Yet these were futures which were partial and ungendered. Adolescence was medicalized and normalized as a 'difficult' stage, with any notion of the pupils developing a gendered and sexual identity carefully erased. In Raschida's case, her status as a blind Muslim woman presented additional problems. This, however, was dealt with by pathologizing her gender and tackling the 'problems' associated with this.

In talking about what lay ahead for the pupils, the teachers emphasized educational goals in terms of academic achievements and social integration. The latter concerned the pupils' successful *performance* of peer interaction, rather than relating equally with them or developing lasting friendships. Teachers envisaged Laura and Susan going to university and obtaining employment, but nothing else. For Raschida, university was a way of avoiding the perils of an arranged marriage in a process of ungendering which will be discussed more fully later in this chapter. Fiona, it was hoped, would obtain work with horses, which staff knew she loved. As for the other pupils, some limited employment was considered possible, but little else was specified for life beyond school. The goal of 'independence', emphasized by Susan's and Graham's teachers, specified them becoming able to look after themselves. Susan was standing in the way of this, according to her teachers, as were her parents, with their over-emphasis on physiotherapy at the expense of academic progress. Graham's parents were also holding him back in his teachers' eyes, and he needed 'time to mature, [being let] a little bit off the leash at home'.

Adolescence had been a difficult time for both Raschida and Laura because of the accompanying loss of vision they had experienced. One learning support teacher described how Laura's experience was entirely typical for pupils at her stage of development:

> She does accept her condition, in fact she accepts it very well to a certain extent but now that she is at puberty, even this thing with the long cane, she doesn't want her friends and her friends' boyfriends to see her with a long cane, so it is a sort of vanity thing and I perfectly understand the whole teenage reaction; she's also having that reaction about everything. They tend to go through a phase like that; she is going through a very difficult time so when a child is going through a stage like that you need to sort of get them through it, talk them out of it really.

Sorting this problem had involved great tenacity and deviousness on the part of her teachers:

> If we decide that a child is having a serious problem and isn't accepting their condition . . . we make a point of sitting down and chatting with the child in an informal way . . . We suggest to the child that we know they are having problems and try and get them to talk about it but if the child won't really talk about it then we just leave it open and say, 'right we are always here' . . . You keep coming back to it every so often . . . It sounds ridiculous because none of us have counselling skills, but you have to wing it. . . . because we see them so often . . . you know when something is wrong with a child, somebody always knows and at that point we then go in and try and find out what it is.

Laura's attempts to avoid attention being drawn to her deteriorating vision had been thwarted by collusion between her teachers and parents:

> With Laura, she tends not to tell us; she is very independent but her parents do . . . That can make it quite difficult because you are trying to solve a problem that you know exists but the child doesn't know that you know. So you are then trying to get the child to tell you about this problem without her realising that you know. We just have to go with the flow but we keep at it.

Adolescence for Raschida had been compounded by her status as a Muslim woman, but one of the specialist teachers had tried to resolve this by pathologizing the problem and seeking external help:

> With Raschida it was weeping and wailing and gnashing of teeth when she started to learn Braille. It was terrible. She was going through difficulties at the time with being a girl and arranged marriages and all sorts of stuff like that, she just saw her whole world coming to an end . . . She was sure they were arranging a marriage for her, they did it for her sister you see and she really didn't want this, so I got onto her psychologist. I mean if there is something like that which is really massive and we don't know how to deal with it we get onto the psychologist and we got him to bring in someone from the Asian women's community secretly . . . [the psychologist] took her out and had a coffee with her and stuff and spoke to her because he had worked in this area before.

Raschida's teachers emphasized the importance of mobility training and learning Braille as a means of being able to move on to University and employment and expressed a wish that her parents would give her the same opportunities as they had given her brother. In Laura's case, the same training was seen as broadening her options, by equipping her with 'the skills . . . to continue on with whatever she chooses to do with her life'. Barry's teachers also considered his adolescence to be problematic, but this was because his increasing weight as he matured had presented 'management problems for his auxiliary'. As was mentioned in Chapter 5, however, Barry seemed to have resolved this by not going to the toilet at school, despite the health problems he risked as a consequence.

Parents and Partial Futures

The parents of the pupils with special needs tended, like their teachers, to silence their gender and sexuality in speaking about their futures. Sometimes this was because they looked only to immediately forthcoming events, such as transferring to primary school or college; in other cases, parents seemed to offer partial accounts of their children's futures in which gender and sexuality was missing. Because of Phillip's uncertain prognosis, his parents refused to look beyond the immediate future. 'We talk about looking ahead but we try not to look too far ahead either because there's not much point in looking at the future, you know, we've got to sort of wait and see just exactly how things develop.' They also mentioned Phillip's fears about his future and his ability to do everything that was expected of him.

Laura's parents had heard from school staff that she was 'university material' but said that 'our biggest worry is her ability to move about'. They recognized that their earlier fears about her mobility within the secondary school had not been realized and hoped that she would be able to cope in a new environment. Nevertheless they felt that their current fears were justified since 'she is not good outside her own environment'. They stressed the importance of 'normality — that's what Laura wants', but did not mention their expectations of life beyond university. Raschida's parents also envisaged her going to university, but were hoping she would select the local one, enabling her to stay at home. 'We worry that she won't manage to look after herself, do her washing. Her mother could do that if she stayed at home. It would be easier for food as she has to eat Halal.' Her parents seemed to question her capacity for independence, voicing concern about her personal well-being. Beyond that, there was no mention of her future prospects.

Sarah's mother said she had 'no idea' about the future. Sarah had been talking to her about nursing, but reckoned that this had been only because she had heard the girl next door mention this and tended to copy her. Peter's mother spoke of having 'no high hopes for him' and described how her sister had been shocked by his (fairly typical) response when she had asked him about his future:

> My sister doesn't know Peter because we're not close or anything and she says 'ah Peter what are you going to do when you leave school?' and he said, 'I'm going to

kill myself' and she was just gobsmacked. But he doesn't know what he's going to do, then, the next thing is, 'I'm going to kill myself. I don't see the point in learning anything because I'm going to kill myself when I leave school' . . . I'm happy enough. It's just up to Peter. If he wants to learn, he'll learn, if he doesn't, he won't. What can you do? You just have to accept it.

Barry's mother indicated that 'he likes ladies and always gets on with them' and praised his current auxiliary as someone who 'knows teenagers', signalling a recognition of Barry's status as an adolescent. Speaking of his future, however, she spoke only of his transfer to secondary school. Scott was also still in primary school and his mother was understandably concerned with the immediate transfer to secondary and the prospect of travelling on the bus. 'I think Scott will find going on the bus, etc., quite harrowing . . . I'll be ill thinking about him going on the bus in case he has a fit, but if it's going to happen it's going to happen, there's nothing you can do about it.' However, she had also thought ahead to what he could achieve in school and hoped that the opportunities to take accredited courses and pursue his interest in music would enable him to qualify for a college course. She described her annoyance at an educational psychologist's patronizing question about what her expectations were for her son, which she had answered tersely: 'just like any other parent's'. Brian's mother also spoke about his transfer to secondary school, expressing some reservations that because he would be going to a special school within a mainstream school and 'he'll see lots of handicapped' people. She also speculated on life beyond school and her concern to avoid him being dependent on her, as she had observed in other families:

I hope he'll remain at school until he's 18, then things will have changed. I'd like him to get some sort of job — maybe as some sort of helper, in gardens, etc. We'd need to be careful about his safety, so we'd need to be sure that he was employed by someone who knows him. Something to get him out of the house. There are two Down's syndrome adults in the village, who are always with their mums. I don't want that for Brian.

Graham's parents suggested that his 'happy-go-lucky nature will see him though life'. They were anxious that he should get a job in order to support himself 'because we won't always be here for him'. His future, as envisaged by his parents, was an independent, but ungendered one with no prospects of relationships or marriage but with perhaps some friendships. However, his parents contended that before all of this was possible, he needed to 'grow up' and hoped that college would encourage this. Fiona's mother hoped she would pursue her interest in horses by taking a college course, but knew that stable management was poorly paid so suggested that she might obtain secretarial work. She made no mention of any other aspect of her daughter's future.

Susan's mother was exceptional in speculating on her daughter's future as possibly including marriage and children. 'She's said she's not going to get married, she's just going to get pregnant [laughs], but I think she'd be the best of mothers, she really would, I'm sure she would be a perfect mother.' More immediately, she envisaged her daughter experiencing some difficult times as an adolescent female. She felt Susan would find this more troublesome than others with different kinds of special needs. 'I think it's harder than for a child that's mentally handicapped because they don't realize the same things like boyfriends, discos and boy talk and that, so I think it's harder for a child that's mentally pretty ok, you know common sense wise.' The advice she had received from professionals, however, had encouraged her to pathologize Susan's experience of adolescence, leading to considerable uncertainty over her future:

> The child psychologist has told us that when she hits the teenage years it's going to be hard for her and he said if she could come out the other end the way she is now, life in front of her could be pretty good, but depending on how she comes out, you know if she gets depressed and not caring for herself or people or whatever.

Despite this gloomy conjecture, Susan's mother had continued to entertain hopes that her daughter would get married and have children:

> I don't know whether there'll be sheltered home accommodation and if she gets married . . . Everyone seems to like her so far and, as I say, if she can keep her personality and her smile, you know she's quite bonny child, hopefully she might get somebody and get married and, hopefully, I can't see any reason why she can't have kids, but we've never actually went into that . . . There's going to be a lot of thinking and working out. I reckon she'd be wasted just to leave school and come home and watch TV for the rest of her life.

As for employment, she said Susan had expressed an interest in physiotherapy, but hoped she would exploit her best asset, her speaking voice, by obtaining a job as a receptionist or as an advocate for others with cerebral palsy.

Transgressive Practices: Engendering the Self

Chapter 4 suggested that the pupils' transgressive practices enabled them to develop new forms of subjectivity. Some of their practices involved the explicit storying of gender and sexuality in their identities and experiences, whereas other activities seemed to suggest more general attempts to challenge the 'social invisibility' (Thomson, 1997: 285) attributed to them. These practices can be read as a form of gender politics which subvert the foundationalist subject (Butler, 1990; Sawicki, 1996) and a 'constant undoing of the categories and gender norms that derive from, and are perpetuated by, sexual *performances*' (Deveux, 1996: 228, original emphasis). The simultaneous challenge of gender, sexuality and disability norms make these practices distinctive and offer new ways of knowing and acting which recognizes the limits imposed by both norms, but also seeks to subvert them.

Raschida revealed how she had hidden her blindness from a boyfriend, by appearing 'blind drunk', until she was no longer able to maintain this pretence. Her boyfriend 'never realized that I couldn't see for ages'. She was only able to do this in an environment which, like school, she knew well, but even then her cover up was elaborate:

> I usually met him at nights and that and he was [drunk] . . . I used to always pretend that I was drunk as well. I [wasn't] really, but I was just saying that so that he'd think, if I couldn't see anything, he'd realize [laughs] . . . I decided to tell him. Because we used to meet up at my friend's house and I knew her house quite well as well, so I never used to bang into things or anything, I'd just act normal, casual.

She eventually told him when she realized she could not keep up the deception. Her anxiety was not just about how he would react to being told that he had been lied to, but how he would feel about her being unable to see and so she worried about 'spoiling things'. 'He couldn't take it, he couldn't believe it . . . It changed things for a while, then we got closer I think in a way, I don't know. It was just better in a way, but I was really worried then.'

Raschida and Laura acknowledged the fragility of their vision as they went through adolescence and Raschida described being upset by her 'dip' in vision and worrying about disclosing this information to her peers:

> I couldn't stop crying . . . [it happened suddenly] in fourth year, a couple of years ago and it was just when I went out with my pal Karen . . . and she couldn't believe it, she thought I was kidding on because she was so used to me being normalish and then all of a sudden it just went worse and then I never used to hang around with my friends . . . I never knew what to tell them. I never wanted to tell them either. Then I think they realized in the classes. I mean I get a teacher in; I never used to like that at all before, when the teacher used to come into the classes. At first, when the teacher used to come in, I couldn't talk to anyone in the class — they used to always stop me from talking, but then they [teachers] got used to the idea and now they talk to the pupils as well.

The boys in Raschida's class had become much more friendly with her once they had got to know her and after she had worked on the kind of knowledge they had of her, they were able to joke with her:

> At the beginning of sixth year some of the boys in the corner never really used to know me and they thought there was something wrong with me, other than my sight, but once I get to know them they're all just pure brand new. They're alright now, they're quite friendly and like they usually, they always say, 'I [saw] you in town and you never waved back'. That's what I always get, but now they realize, they're always just slagging me off.

Peter said that he had a girlfriend in the school and offered to point her out in the playground, providing her identity remained secret. Further questioning seemed to suggest that the girl was unaware of her status but that he was working on this. Susan indicated that she would like to have a child, but not necessarily in wedlock. This comment followed a class discussion in which she pronounced that 'all men are rubbish', but she also said she got on well with all of the boys in the class and they liked her. In Chapter 4 it was suggested that both Susan and Peter appeared to transgress into disability, yet they seemed to be seeking an active version of gender and sexuality, by indicating their potential for relationships. Each of these actions and comments seemed to inscribe gender and sexuality into the pupils' identities and experiences in ways which their mainstream peers, teachers and parents had avoided.

Other transgressive practices by the pupils, discussed in Chapter 4, challenged the social invisibility associated with disability by working on the coercive markers of disability which constrained them to be both disabled and ungendered. Objects, such as the long cane or the hearing aid were shunned because they were visible markers of disability. Routines signalling disability were avoided, such as, in Barry's case going to the toilet with his auxiliary; or events were planned ahead by Phillip to enable him to participate in ways which did not highlight his disability. The pupils also worked on the coercive aspects of their mainstream peers' governmental regime, for example, Raschida and Laura tried to make their peers less 'uptight'. The governmental regime of Graham and Brian's peers, in which they assumed responsibility for their pastoral care and their pedagogic development, infantilized them and seemed to close off options to inscribe gender and sexuality into their own identities. This reinforced their social invisibility and disqualified them from peer relationships. Brian's overtly friendly behaviour crossed the boundaries of contact between pupils and could be read as an act of inscribing gender and sexuality into his own identity. Yet, his peers did not read it in any way other than an as example of the typical exuberance of a pupil with Down's Syndrome and an another opportunity to support his development by encouraging him to wash his face before he kissed anyone.

Foucault's 'box of tools' (1977a: 208) has made it possible to analyse the way in which the identities and experiences of pupils with special needs have been constructed for them, by peers, teachers and others, and resisted through their transgressive practices. When it comes to gender and sexuality, Foucault has been criticized for abandoning 'the idea of the body as a sensuous potentiality' (Turner, 1984: 250). Foucault's ideas have been seen as irrelevant, particularly to women, because of his male-oriented perspective and almost contemptuous disregard of women's interests (Butler, 1990; MacCannell and MacCannell, 1993; Soper, 1993) whereas others have simply considered his work unhelpful. Moi, for example, has suggested that the price of succumbing to Foucault's analysis is the 'depoliticisation of feminism . . . caught up in a sado-masochistic spiral of power and resistance . . . in which it will be quite impossible to argue that women under patriarchy constitute an oppressed group, let alone develop a theory of their liberation' (1985: 95).

Other feminists have considered Foucault to have relevance to their work, and Deveux (1996) highlights three waves of feminist interest in Foucault, focusing on docile bodies and the exercise of self-surveillance (Bartky, 1988); agonistic resistance

(Sawicki, 1988); and sexual identity and regimes of truth and power (Butler, 1990). Bailey (1993: 102) suggests that Foucault's 'refusal of the notions of the trans-historical and stable categories of sexuality/sex' has value for feminists, whereas Ramazanoglu (1993) contends that feminists cannot afford to ignore his theories. Foucauldian analyses of women's experiences of anorexia (Bordo, 1989) the fashion and beauty industry (Bartky, 1990), violence (MacCannell and MacCannell, 1993) and identity and difference (see Benabib, 1990; Braidotti, 1991; Hartsock, 1990) signal a new understanding of power/knowledge relationships and the self among feminists, lured by the 'tantalising promise of bodies . . . with partial interested truths [which] allow for fragmented identities, partial strategies and specific, interested strategies' (Bailey, 1993: 107). Haraway has given this new configuration of political identity the name of 'cyborg' (1991: 176), an undecidable image which fuses boundaries between human, animal and machine. The cyborg both defies single categories and recognizes its complicity in their construction, freeing individuals from 'the need to root politics in identification, vanguard parties, purity and mothering' (ibid.).

Foucault's interest in transgression initially focused on sexuality and the paradoxical situation in which individuals found themselves where their bodies and their sexuality were subject to interdictions, yet they were forced to tell the truth about themselves as sexual beings. Foucault's *History of Sexuality*, therefore, developed as an inquiry which asked, 'how had the subject been compelled to decipher himself in regard to what was forbidden?' (1988a: 17). Foucault has clearly not ignored gender and sexuality as some of his critics have suggested; indeed his own transgressive practices were directed at sexual acts (Miller, 1993; Simons, 1995) in which the eroticization of power and strategic relations (Foucault, 1984d) in sado-masochism was experienced as a practical transgression of limits (Simons, 1995). The pupils' transgressive practices did not displace disability, gender and sexuality, an outcome which would be neither feasible nor desirable, but promoted new knowledge of their experiences as disabled, gendered and sexual subjects. Kolodny (cited in Sawicki, 1996) suggests that these new forms of subjectivity offer individuals a kind of freedom that is marked by the 'fluidity, reversibility and mutability of relations of power — that individuals in one society enjoy relative to another' (Sawicki, 1996: 175). There is clearly a need for more detailed analyses of transgressive practices which relate specifically to gender and sexuality. The final part of this chapter explores how disabled men and women have challenged the desexing discourses of disability and have 'come out' as gendered individuals with sexual identities.

Coming out as Gendered Subjects

The silencing of the gender and sexuality of disabled people is a complex process, which, on the one hand infantilizes and dehumanizes disabled people, rendering them passive and asexual (Shakespeare et al., 1996), and on the other hand seeks to protect them from sexual knowledge within a discourse of prohibition and risk

(Banim and Guy, cited in Shakespeare et al., 1996). Shildrick and Price note how the silencing of sexuality among disabled women paradoxically engenders their broken bodies as feminine in terms of dependency and passivity. Moreover, the body becomes a focus for self-surveillance whereby 'the objectifying gaze of the human sciences, which fragments and divides the body against itself, has its counterpart in personal in-sight which equally finds the body untrustworthy and in need of governance' (1996: 104). Disabled gay men and lesbian women have often found the disability movement intolerant of homosexuality and the 'body fascism' (Shakespeare et al., 1996) within the gay community oppressive. Consequently, they have felt rejected by both disabled and homosexual communities.

Coming out as gendered individuals with a sexuality is a fundamental right of disabled individuals, and acquiring sexual citizenship (Plummer, 1995) is simply an extension of the rights of all individuals to citizenship in civil, political and social terms. This may, however, be characterized more by 'panic and extreme anxiety' than by pride (Corbett, 1996: 98). Corbett argues that pride comes much later with 'the strength that an open and receptive approach to life can bring' (1996: 99), and although she is talking about coming out as a lesbian, she has drawn parallels between disability politics and gay pride (Corbett, 1994). According to Marks (1996), gender and sexuality may be articulated with disability in three ways: marriage and parenting, women performing unwaged work, and homosexuality. Each of these is likely to be problematic because when disabled people 'assert their rights to sexual lives they heighten their visibility rather than increase their chances of integration and acceptance' (Brown, 1994: 124). Marks (1996) attributes this problem to the ways in which social movements such as feminism and gay pride have failed to take account of the needs of disabled people, whereas Corbett urges gay disabled people to speak up and force the gay community to take notice, since 'pride has to be audible and visible' (1994: 347). Finger (1992) criticizes disabled people for failing to challenge this aspect of their oppression:

> Sexuality is often the source of our deepest oppression; it is also often the source of our deepest pain. It's easier for us to talk about — and formulate strategies for changing — discrimination in employment, education, and housing than to talk about our exclusion from sexuality and reproduction. (Finger, 1992: 9)

Morris (1993) points out that all oppressed groups need allies and suggests that feminists can help disabled women, but Ballard argues that feminists must also examine the lack of disabled researchers and academics and 'the absence of disabled people's own definitions and analysis from feminist work and from our culture in general' (1997: 252).

The disability movement presents a significant barrier to the acquisition of a gendered and sexual identity by disabled people by disregarding the body in accounts of disability (Hughes and Paterson, 1997). Oliver's assertion that 'disablement has nothing to do with the body' (1996: 35) is an attempt to foreground the political task of the social model to tackle oppression, and Finkelstein (1996) has argued that considerations of personal experience and impairment are likely to dilute the effectiveness of the social model. These writers have sought to erase dissent from within the disability movement and speak with a unified voice which will 'challenge the continuing complacency of the intellectual establishment and . . . win the battle for a social model understanding of society and our lives' (Shakespeare and Watson, 1997: 299). Such unity has proved impossible since not everyone has accepted the need to remove the body and impairment from the debate. Morris, for example, is critical of the social model's tendency to 'deny the experience of our own bodies' (1991: 10) whereas Casling expresses dissatisfaction with the 'rigid genealogy of disability thinking' (1993: 200). Hughes and Paterson regard the efforts to ignore the body in disability studies as ironic, given that 'the body has become fashionable' (1997: 328) elsewhere, for example in sociology. In Kundura's terms, the removal of the body from the social model amounts to a 'rape of privacy' (1986: 111) in which disabled people are forced to live a 'life without secrets' (1986: 110), without their own bodies.

Plummer (1995) and Shakespeare et al. (1996) argue that personal narratives, explored within their local and more global contexts, can force the non-disabled world to recognize and value disabled people's sexuality. It can also encourage the disability movement to prioritize these matters (Shakespeare et al., 1996). Most importantly, however, it sends a message to disabled people which affirms their identities as gendered and sexual subjects:

> It offers disabled people themselves, as individuals, validation for their own sexual stories, for their own experiences, both positive and negative. We *can* talk about sex. We can *have* sex — we *are* entitled to have sex and find love. We *do* face oppression, abuse and prejudice, but we can fight back and we can demand support and the space to heal. (1996: 207, original emphasis)

Chapter 9

Inclusion as Ethical Work on Ourselves

There's an optimism that consists in saying that things couldn't be better. My optimism would consist rather in saying that so many things can be changed, fragile as they are, bound up more with circumstances than necessities, more arbitrary than self evident, more a matter of complex, but temporary, historical circumstances than of inevitable anthropological constraints . . . You know, to say that we are much more recent than we think, is to place at the disposal of the work that we do on ourselves the greatest possible share of what is presented to us as inaccessible. (Foucault, 1988e: 156)

This book began by taking to task those researchers whose theories and practices have mythologized a sense of progress in relation to pupils with special needs. It was suggested that researchers' unwillingness to address the power relationships within which research knowledge is produced has maintained the binary divide between researcher and researched, thereby ensuring that research continues to be seen as a 'violation' and 'irrelevant' by disabled people (Oliver, 1992a: 105). Furthermore, researchers' failure to theorize was criticized for doing untold damage to the project of inclusion, allowing it to become no more than 'a new language for functionalism' (Slee, 1998: 130). This bleak picture has provoked Barton to ask whether the notion of inclusive education is 'romantic, subversive or realistic' (1997: 231).

The accounts provided by the pupils with special needs and their mainstream peers present a much more sanguine view of inclusion which does not hold to a utopian 'vision', yet recognizes the place of 'struggle' (Barton 1997: 239). The power relationships in which the pupils were enmeshed were much more subtle and were often positive and creative. Raschida, Laura and the others were not the passive objects of special needs knowledge upon whom inclusion was practised, but were *actively seeking inclusion*, working on themselves and their mainstream peers to make inclusion happen. Their transgressive strategies, practised amid the threat of coercive markers of disability from multiple sources, enabled them to defy the identities and experiences chosen for them and to practise alternative forms of conduct. The mainstream pupils, with their highly nuanced understanding of disability and of matters of justice and equality, played a key role as gatekeepers, within their mini-regime of governmentality. This appeared mostly to support the inclusion of pupils with special needs through their pastoral care and pedagogic strategies. At the same time, however, the pupils' ambivalences and uncertainties, where they felt 'uptight' or sorry for the pupils with special needs, also provided coercive markers of disability. From the informal discourses, inclusion can be read as a messy and unstable process which the mainstream pupils both sanction and prohibit.

This leaves everyone — pupils with special needs, mainstream pupils, teachers, schools and researchers — with a great deal to do. As Simons points out, the responsibilities are 'awesome' (1995: 123). It requires the kind of ethical work on our selves and our practices which is guided by an underlying telos, in which everyone should strive towards self-mastery (Blacker, 1998) and a set of principles which 'tell you in each situation, and in some way spontaneously, how you should behave' (Foucault, 1987a: 117). According to Foucault, this involves challenging 'the evidence and the postulates, of shaking up habits, ways of acting and thinking, of dispelling commonplace beliefs, of taking a new measure of rules and institutions' (1991b: 11–12). He argues for the development of 'a critical ontology of ourselves' (1984b: 50), which allows for the analysis of, and experimentation on, limits imposed upon us. Foucault conceives of this as an attitude or way of life, in which individuals recognize the limits imposed upon them but also seek to test these limits. Disabled people, therefore, might recognize their disability as imposing certain intractable limits upon them but might also challenge artificially created barriers such as attitudes.

According to Foucault (1977c), limits are both transgressible and immutable, crossable in the sense that they can be challenged through practices which promote alternative subjectivities, and uncrossable, in that they cannot be removed permanently or transcended. Thus, work on limits cannot be reduced to political success (Bernaur, 1988). The conundrum of the uncrossable limit (Boyne, 1990) has led Foucault to conclude that the efficacy of transgression lies in the confusion of crossing/uncrossing and the knowledge that the limit itself has no limit. Even once we grasp the sense of our imbrication in the power/knowledge networks, however, 'the thought of further excess remains' (Boyne, 1990: 81). This means that the work on limits never succeeds and always remains to be done. Simons suggests that this work 'creates political fictions with the self-conscious awareness that it does so, while also being aware that the political *facts* created by other theories are also fictions' (1995: 123, original emphasis). The work we do on ourselves is always critical of self and others and thereby 'avoids the pitfalls of narcissistic aestheticism and the alienation of political obsession' (Blacker, 1998: 363). Inclusion, then, is a precarious process, in which 'risk and promise are necessary conditions for each other' (Simons, 1995: 123). It should be guided by 'suspicion, always, but never condemnation, the latter being merely the mirror image of utopianism' (Blacker, 1998: 364).

The Foucauldian project of ethical work has some parallels with the critical pedagogy offered by Giroux (1988; 1992), McLaren (1995) and others. Both set out to create 'responsive landscapes or spaces' (Shotter, 1997) which privilege the normally subjugated voice of the pupil and introduce 'failure, loss, confusion, unease [and] limitation' for dominant groups (Jones, 1998: 25). In each case the teacher establishes dialogue which seeks to break the 'culture of silence' (McLaren, 1995: 32) and traverse the boundaries of difference. Spatial metaphors such as margin and centre are deployed with the aim of moving individuals to a more politically effective space.

There are, however, three important distinctions between critical pedagogy and the Foucauldian ethical project of inclusion. First, the ethical project recognizes that the demand for narrative can become part of a renewal of colonizing power (Bhabha, 1994; Jones, 1998) and a 'strategy of surveillance and exploitation' (Bhabha, 1994: 99). These instances of the 'ferocious standardising benevolence' of the 'relentless recognition of the Other' (Spivak, 1988: 294) become, therefore, little more than acts of voyeurism by dominant groups (Jones, 1998). Those engaged in the ethical project, in contrast, understand that their own 'cannibal desire to *know the other* through being taught/fed by her is simultaneously a refusal to know' (1998: 21, original emphasis). Thus, the privileging of speaking within the ethical project gives way to the act of hearing what the speaker says (Jones, 1998).

The ethical project also differs from critical pedagogy in its refusal to offer promises of rescue, 'escape routes to the grounds of certainty' (Stronach and Maclure, 1997: 9). Within critical pedagogy, these gestures take a variety of forms, including moves to 'get back finally to reality, history, society, politics' (Derrida, 1990: 79); alternatively, they involve appeals to pluralism using the grammar of spatial rescue and becoming together (McLaren, 1995), appealing to a kind of consensus in which members agree to differ. Finally, they might involve some kind of futuring, such as the one Skrtic offers special education:

> And, of course, the aim of deconstructing special education is to clear the way for special educators to reconstruct it in a manner that is more consistent with the ideal of serving the best educational and political interests of their consumers . . . reconstructing public education as an integrative system is a distributive good that serves the best moral, political, and economic interests of all Americans. (1995: 233–4)

One might be surprised that Skrtic chose to save only American democracy, given his faith in the potential for salvation. Such an agenda, however, is 'both impossible and pointless', since it is inevitably 'half-baked', concealed by the notion of 'emergence' (Stronach and Maclure, 1997: 151). The implication of everyone in ethical work — pupils with special needs, mainstream pupils, teachers, schools and researchers — articulates their complicity in exclusion and their responsibility for inclusion. The ethical project seeks to create spaces for dialogue, where individuals can also work across boundaries (McLaren, 1995), but acknowledges that these spaces can be oppressive. Practitioners of the ethical project avoid futuring inclusion, preferring to turn their attention to the past and the way inclusion has been fictionalized. Rescue gestures are avoided, although it is recognized that the appeal to human agency could be read as such and that there is possibly a hint of universalist normativity implicit in the notion of the ethically stylized individual (Smart, 1998).

The final feature which distinguishes the ethical project from critical pedagogy is that there is no emancipatory goal, promising freedom and empowerment to its subjects. It avoids emancipatory politics, 'created out of empathy for others by means of a passionate connection through difference' (McLaren, 1995: 106) and premised on a 'touching faith in the *talking cure* of story-telling' (Jones, 1998: 12) to enable subjects to participate equally. Instead, an ethical project allows individuals to strive for 'the self reflective goal of experiencing the self as agent' (Warren, 1988: 138) and knowledge of the self in relation to constraints. Foucault argues that the ethical project offers more than emancipation from external or internal constraint by allowing individuals to fight the battle of 'self over self' (1987b: 91). 'Self mastery' (p. 92) produces a particular kind of active freedom, which Pignatelli describes as 'inventive, resourceful, strategical moves along an axis of power, moves which possibly anticipate but cannot terminate the play of power' (1993: 427).

Foucault's framework for ethical work on ourselves focuses on 'the forms of relations with the self, on the methods and techniques by which he works them out, on the exercises by which he makes of himself an object to be known, and on the practices that enable him to transform his own mode of being' (1987b: 30). As Smart points out, Foucault gave little advice on how to achieve this. He mentions the role of the counsellor, friend, guide or master 'who will tell you the truth about yourself' (1998: 82), but does not discuss the nature of the relationships involved. Ethical work has four dimensions, which Foucault (1987b) elaborates upon in relation to sexuality:

1   Determination of the ethical substance: this involves identifying 'this or that part of oneself as prime material of his moral conduct' (1987b: 26) and allowing individuals to decide which aspect of the self is to be worked on. Foucault offers fidelity as an example, with individuals resisting temptation or experiencing the intensity of a binding relationship.

2   The mode of subjection concerns the 'way in which the individual establishes his relationship to the rule and recognizes himself as obliged to put it into practice' (1987b: 27). Foucault argues that this allows the individual to pursue 'brilliance, beauty, nobility or perfection' (1987b: 27). Blacker (1998) suggests that an example of this is the Greek aristocrat who fashions his diet according to certain aesthetic criteria.

3   Self-practice or ethical work involves what one does 'not only in order to bring one's conduct into compliance with a given rule, but to attempt to transform oneself into the ethical subject of one's behaviour' (1987b: 27). Thus, sexual austerity, in Foucault's example, can be practised silently, through thought or involving a much more explicit and 'relentless combat' (1987b: 27). It is a form of 'asceticism' (Blacker, 1998: 362) through which individuals transform themselves.

4   The *Telos* is the ultimate goal which an individual is trying to achieve and in Foucault's example, fidelity is associated with an aspiration towards complete self mastery. Blacker describes this as a kind of 'controlled and self-regulated dissemination of the subject into the world, a positive dissolution . . . not self-absorption, but being absorbed into the world: a *losing–finding* of the self' (1998: 362–3, original emphasis).

Foucault argues that one should become so accomplished in this ethical work that it is done unconsciously: 'You must have learned principles so firmly that when your desires, your appetites or your fears awaken like barking dogs, the *logos* will speak with the voice of a master who silences the dogs by a single command (1987a: 117, original emphasis).

Although Foucault's ethical work is directed towards a kind of sexual austerity, it can be applied to inclusion in a much more positive way, privileging, rather than suppressing, desires. To take Raschida as an example, it is possible to specify elements of the ethical project in the work she was already doing on herself and to envisage ways of extending it. The *determination of her ethical substance* could identify disability as the part of herself to be worked on. It is just as important to indicate which aspect is not to be addressed and Raschida might omit her ethnicity as requiring less work of this kind. Her *mode of subjection* could involve analysing the disabling barriers she faces and the discourses through which she is forced to be disabled. She might also specify the extent to which the mainstream pupils and teachers enable and constrain her, giving her material from which to determine the kind of *self practice or ethical work* she wishes to do. In contrast with the Foucauldian asceticism, Raschida's self-work might focus on strategies for easy movement around school, practising a kind of nonchalance in her relations with her peers. Her ethical work is also likely to focus on her peers' governmental regime, as her accounts suggested she had already done, but might also tackle some of the teachers' practices and attitudes. Finally, the act of spelling out a goal or *telos* is useful in itself as a means of helping others to understand Raschida's desires and her notion of self-mastery might include efficiency in her movement and acceptance by her friends. Work of this kind could produce lives which are 'larger, more active, more affirmative and richer in possibilities' (Deleuze, 1988: 92).

This work on the promotion of new subjectivities (Foucault, 1982) is not just ethical, but is also political, social and philosophical and is put into practice through a kind of 'curiosity', which

> evokes the care of what exists and might exist; a sharpened sense of reality, but one that is never immobilized before it; a readiness to find what surrounds us strange and odd; a certain determination to throw off familiar ways of thought and to look at the same things in a different way . . . a lack of respect for the traditional hierarchies of what is important and fundamental. (Foucault, 1988e: 321)

It requires to be done by everyone, but since government of self and others is linked (Foucault, 1984e), it will be necessary to establish conduct which 'seeks the rules of acceptable behaviour in relations with others' Foucault (1988a: 22). According to Levinas, 'I have to respond to and for the Other without occupying myself with the Other's responsibility in my regard' (1987: 137). Foucault regrets that the self can no longer be allowed to predominate as it did in the ancient Greek sense in which 'the principal work of art which one has to take care of, the main area to which one must apply aesthetic values, is oneself, one's life, one's existence' (1984a: 362). Smart (1998) suggests that the contemporary version of caring for oneself, characterized by self-determination, self-expression and hedonism, has led to indifference towards the other, but this was not apparent in the relationships described by the pupils. The work which each of the individuals already involved in the processes of inclusion and exclusion may do on themselves is discussed in the context of their responsibilities both to themselves and others.

The Ethical Project of Inclusion

Pupils with Special Needs

If mainstream pupils, teachers, schools and researchers are all engaged in ethical work on themselves, they will remove much of the oppression normally experienced by disabled people. As Foucault points out, these actions are linked to the techniques for the directions of others (1984a: 370), suggesting that within educational establishments 'one is managing others and teaching them to manage themselves' (ibid.). Consequently, there may be less need for the kind of defensive strategies which the pupils reported in this research, where 'the constant fear of discovery makes *normative* social interaction difficult and adds to the barriers faced by disabled people' (Barnes, 1996a: 43, original emphasis). As French points out, however, social remedies can never 'truly eliminate disability' (1993a: 19) and others (see Oliver, 1987; Finkelstein, 1990) have commented on the unsuccessful efforts to remove barriers created by public attitudes. That is not to say that these should not continue to be tackled; it is also clear, however, that pupils need to be helped to cope with the real situations in which they find themselves and to seek ways of overcoming the disabling barriers which remain. They may need some encouragement to explore the possibilities of being active subjects, with options to transgress. In this research, Brian, Sarah, Graham and Scott, each of whom had cognitive difficulties, seemed to have fewer opportunities to transgress than the other pupils, but this need not necessarily be the case if teachers support them and if mainstream pupils loosen the grip of their governmental regime. Booth and Ainscow have suggested that singling out pupils using professionally derived labels of special needs or SEN could 'further contribute to their marginalisation' (1998a: 67). This is a naïve view, which ignores the political context of disability and the need to help individuals to negotiate the double bind of challenging subjectification as constructed subjects (Ligget, 1988), acknowledging the binarisms of special/ normal or disabled/able-bodied in order to speak against them.

The ethical work by pupils with special needs might concern how their disabilities are perceived by others, narrating their identity in order to make it live (Brannigan, 1996). Individuals may choose to work away from disability, as Raschida, Laura and Barry did in their transgressive practices, work towards it, like Susan and Peter, or do both, as Phillip seemed to prefer (Chapter 4). Teachers might help pupils to explore their sense of self — expressed as desires rather than needs — and to analyse the constraining and enabling factors, but should avoid passing judgments on them. This could then lead to the removal of some constraints or the enunciation of strategies to circumvent others. Teachers could also specify the kind of support they perceive to be necessary, with both parties exploring the consequences of receiving this kind of support or doing without it. It may be possible to negotiate strategies which recognize both needs and desires, for example, by providing support within classrooms which does not disturb peer interaction. Dialogue of this kind may encourage pupils to 'escape the grasp of categories' (Foucault, 1977d: 190) and practise alternative forms of conduct. At the same time, however, they can be helped to understand the consequences of certain actions, such as doing without specialist help or becoming dependent on one's peers. The point is 'not to abolish identity (or subjectivity) but to transform the way in which we experience identity' (Simons, 1995: 121).

Ethical work for pupils with special needs privileges their desires over professionally constructed needs, but 'this means not what we most powerfully desire, but which desires we most identify with or most value' (Magill, 1997: 71). This work also recognizes that knowledge about their needs is also an instrument of power which is constraining and disabling. Although there is much work which individuals might do to tackle these constraints, such as helping mainstream peers to be less 'uptight', other limits may be more intractable. Greater knowledge of the way these limits are constructed, that is by a disabling society, may move individuals towards collective, rather than individual, transgressions, but it is important that they are given the scope to make these kinds of decisions. There is a danger that helping pupils with special needs to develop transgressive practices which relate specifically to them merely recreates the binarism of *the included child*, who is always identifiable. This need not be the case if everyone is recognized as doing ethical work on themselves, on their 'fragile *shaggy* hybridic identities' (McRobbie, 1994: 192, original emphasis); this work will vary for everyone, according to their priorities and goals. Thus, everyone has to learn to 'live in and with selves divided in and through incommensurable difference' (Kelly, 1997: 122), learning to 'consolidate oneself as a subject of lack' (Silverman, 1996: 37).

Mainstream Pupils

The mainstream pupils' accounts suggested a commitment to the welfare of pupils with special needs and an engagement with inclusion. Their ethical work, therefore, might work towards greater self consciousness of their governmental regime, focusing on its positive aspects and on the avoidance of activities which promote exclusion. Connelly suggests that the antagonism which may emerge through resentment of the other can be converted to 'agonistic respect', in which 'each party comes to appreciate the extent to which its self-definition is bound up with the other and . . . opponents can become bonded together, partially and contingently, through an enhanced experience of the contestability of the problematic each pursues most fervently' (1998: 122). Respect is, thus, more far-reaching than mere liberal tolerance — 'a passive letting the other be' (ibid.) and opens up the space for negotiating difference 'by identifying traces in the other of the sensibility one identifies in oneself and locating in the self elements of the sensibility attributed to the other' (1998: 123). This could, of course, be read as another brand of utopian rhetoric. On the other hand, it could be seen as reconfiguring the already there governmental regime, in which the mainstream pupils had determined their own responsibilities with regard to inclusion.

The very positive aspects of the mainstream pupils' regime, such as their pedagogic involvement with pupils with special needs, could be reinforced, encouraging them to examine their responsibilities towards pupils with special needs and to push the limits of these responsibilities still further. They might also scrutinize the ambivalences and contradictions within their understanding of disability and identity, not with a view to eradicating these, but in order to reach decisions about their conduct and its consequences. For example, they might consider how charity discourses, expressed as feeling sorry for individuals, disable them by making them passive, and contribute to the oppression of disabled people generally. Respect, in this context, arises from 'an indebtedness to those who prevent limits from congealing by sustaining the contest between different ideas and policies' (Connelly, cited in Simons, 1995: 121). Brian's mainstream peers signalled their need for help in coping with behaviour which breached their usual rules about physical contact and sexuality. This could be done in the context of general discussions about sexuality.

The significance of mainstream pupils as inclusion gatekeepers should not be underestimated. This research highlighted the positive and supportive aspect of their involvement, and their assumption that inclusion is an inalienable right, but also suggested that they could be highly negative and punitive, finding ways of legitimizing the exclusion of individuals. Mainstream pupils could be encouraged to work on their governmental regime, emphasizing the positive, rather than negative, aspects. Ethical work of this kind could also help to give pupils a greater sense of their active engagement with school processes, rather than as passive recipients.

Teachers

Foucault argues that in order to do ethical work on the self 'one must listen to the teachings of a master' (1987a: 118). The findings from this research, however, suggest that these teachings are flawed and that teachers have extensive ethical work to do, in scrutinizing how their own practices disable individuals, albeit unintentionally. Pignatelli urges teachers, above all, to 'avoid discourse-practices that essentialize categories of deviance in the minds of pupils and themselves; discourse-practices that cause pupils to internalize and monitor their deviant status — in effect blaming themselves for their own marginality' (1993: 420).

Teachers and other professionals have ethical work to do on themselves, in order to avoid using experience as 'terrorism' on those without it (Spivak, 1994: 129), while also facilitating their pupils' ethical work. Felman suggests that the biggest challenge for professionals comes from their own 'passion for ignorance':

> Teaching . . . has to deal not so much with lack of knowledge as with resistances to knowledge. Ignorance . . . is a *passion* inasmuch as traditional pedagogy postulated a desire for knowledge — an analytically informed pedagogy has to reckon with *the passion for ignorance*. Ignorance, in other words, is nothing other than a desire to ignore . . . It is not a simple lack of information but the incapacity — or the refusal — to acknowledge one's own implication in the information. (1982: 30, original emphasis)

The teachers in this research seemed to demonstrate regularly such a passion for ignorance with regard to the pupils with special needs. This was not because they lacked compassion or were unprofessional; rather, their discourse of needs encouraged them to blank out some of the pupils' desires, such as Raschida's reluctance to use a long cane, Fiona's dislike of her hearing aid or Susan's enjoyment of her peers' attention. There have been many calls for a scrutiny of professional knowledge (see Skrtic, 1995; Tomlinson, 1996) and of teachers' 'interests and investments in the knowledge being forged' (Orner, 1998: 279). Skrtic (1995) argues that the process of professionalization creates individuals who share the belief that they are acting in the best interests of clients, based on knowledge which they assume to be objective. Ethical work by teachers, therefore, involves subverting their own 'ideology of expertism' (Troyna and Vincent, 1996: 142).

Lowson (1994) offers a useful deconstructive strategy in this respect, by inviting professionals to pathologize themselves as suffering from Professional Thought Disorder (PTD). This condition has a number of features, including a compulsion to analyse and categorize the experience of others; disordered cognition, which manifests itself in rigidly held beliefs; delusions of grandeur; and negative transference and projection, in which the sufferers cannot 'distinguish their own wishes and impulses from those of the people they wish to be helping' (cited in Corbett, 1996: 40). When professional language is turned back towards the professionals themselves, the effect is 'distinctly sinister' (ibid.). Yet, scrutiny of their own clinical symptoms, for example, as a staff development activity, could encourage teachers and other professionals to recognize and remove the 'rigidity, imperviousness and defensiveness' (ibid.) in their language and practices. Pupils with special needs and others who have to endure such behaviour from professionals may be helped by understanding the etymology of PTD and the symptoms which force professionals to act in certain ways.

Kelly suggests that teachers might 'grasp difference as a pedagogical project' (1997: 113), aspiring to a missing, rather than a meeting, of minds (Johnston, 1977). Greene argues that students must experience opportunities to 'articulate the themes of their own existence', experiencing 'curriculum as possibility' (1978: 18). Schaafsma (1998) proposes the use of fictional strategies in which pupils produce narratives which enable them to explore identity, difference and the power relations within the classroom. At the same time, however, teachers should not subject pupils to a will to confess, as this is a disciplinary technique in itself (Foucault, 1976; Orner, 1998). Critical fictions are 'both a struggle against the privileges of knowledge and opposition against mystifying representations imposed on people, and also still constructed to some extent in and through the technologies of power' (Schaafsma, 1998: 267). Through these processes, teachers can help pupils to recognize 'the constitutive force of discourse' (p. 257), recognizing the multiplicity and ambiguity of these discourses but also realizing that these are not 'totally determining'. Personal and Social Development is an obvious part of the curriculum for these activities, but there are other areas such as English where identity and difference could easily be a focus. Teachers can offer pupils feedback on their personal fictions which raises their consciousness of possibilities of further work on their limits, whatever these may be. This allows teachers to fulfil their obligations to pupils, which Fendler suggests 'consists of teaching the soul — including fears, attitudes, will and desire' (1998: 55).

It might have seemed that teachers have been portrayed as the villains of this research story. They did at times appear insensitive to the desires of pupils with special needs and unaware of the gatekeeping potential of the mainstream pupils. Yet they were merely operating within a professional discourse which had its own integrity and rules of conduct and which had the capacity to silence the pupils' discourses. This is not intended as yet another opportunity to berate teachers, but merely to invite them to examine how their practices might disable pupils and to make space within their professional discourse of needs for their pupils' desires.

Schools

Schools also have a great deal to do and their ethical project will necessarily be far-reaching, if they are to become less oppressive spaces for pupils with special needs. A major task, therefore, has to be effecting 'deep changes in the way schools work' (Pignatelli, 1993: 411). Slee (1996) suggests that schools should pathologize themselves in order to acknowledge their own failures. This would expose the ways in which special needs has been used as a 'bureaucratic device for dealing with the complications arising from clashes between narrow, waspish curricula and disabled students' (Slee, 1998: 131–2). Disability has to be seen in terms of uneven power relations and privilege and speaks to 'political, rather than individual pathologies' (1998: 134).

School policies on discipline and bullying could accentuate the positive role of pupils in caring for themselves and others, at the same time indicating that negative behaviour will not be tolerated. Sharp and Thomson (1997) argue that all staff and students should be involved in the formulation of anti-bullying policies to ensure that all have an investment in its success. Anti-bullying strategies, aimed at sparing all pupils the 'oppression and repeated intentional humiliation implied in bullying' (Olweus, 1994: 1183), should avoid entrenching further the pupils' disabled identities. Greater alertness by teachers, to situations such as the victimization which left Sarah in tears, the names which Scott had to endure and the vulnerability of Peter at his new school might have enabled them to intervene constructively.

The application of school effectiveness research to special education has already proved seductive for some (Ainscow, 1991; Ramasut and Reynolds, 1993), even though, according to Reynolds, the findings 'may cast doubt on the validity and practical value of the [inclusionist] enterprise' (1995: 121). Gerber explores the possibility that the efforts of a school to raise the achievement of disabled students may have little or no impact on a schools' mean performance outcomes and concludes that there are 'serious implications for the concept of school effectiveness' (1996: 170). Booth is right to dismiss such an approach as 'expensively misconceived' (1998: 87), on the grounds that what it has to say about effective schools 'could be agreed in an afternoon by experienced teachers pooling their ideas' (ibid.). Slee's suspicion of attempts to 'deploy effective schooling research as a way of collapsing the special needs conundrum into the general mission of school improvement' (1998: 130) is also well placed. Pupils with special needs stand to lose most from the school effectiveness mentality because it forces teachers to demonstrate that their disproportionate expenditure on them, in terms of money and effort, has been productive (Bataille, 1985) and creates a normalizing and differentiating imperative. There is a need to exercise deep scepticism in the direction of these particular fictions, which Hamilton (1996) has labelled as 'an ethnocentric pseudo-science that serves merely to mystify anxious administrators and marginalise classroom practitioners', and which will inevitably be detrimental to inclusion.

Ethical work for schools focuses, of course, on everyone in it — teachers, senior management, ancillary staff and pupils — but also addresses the schools' institutionalized practices. A responsiveness to diversity and avoidance of disabling practices could help pupils with special needs to feel valued. These measures could help to develop schools as communities in which there is 'openness to unassimilated otherness' (Young 1990b, 1990: 319). The notion of community is itself problematic, because it is prefaced on notions of unity and consensus (Bauman, 1996; Young, 1990b) and fails to 'square the circle' (Bauman, 1996: 79) between community membership and self determination. That is, it fails to recognize how individuals can be active agents responsible for themselves and others within a community. The ethical project for schools incorporates both personal and collective responsibility, with individuals establishing the rules of conduct for themselves and in relation to others.

Researchers

Researchers' ethical work might be devoted to scrutiny of the ways in which closure in their own thinking is disabling and how truths about progress in integration and inclusion have been 'arbitrarily mass manufactured and disseminated' (Blacker, 1998: 357). Smart suggests that what is needed is a 'critical examination of the various ways in which we have come to govern ourselves and others through the articulation of a distinction between truth and falsity' (1986: 171). This requires researchers to turn their attention to knowledge production. The ethical project also demands that researchers look at their own complicity in this process. Blacker (1998) suggests that ethical work has two guiding principles of 'efficacy' and 'honesty' (1998: 359). Individuals achieve efficacy by narrowing the scope of their activity and thereby widening and deepening its potential consequences. Specialization should, therefore, be privileged over generalization. Honesty requires individuals to be attentive to the consequences of their theorizing and maintain the effort required to be vigilant. Blacker insists this does not entail searching for the *truth* about oneself, but 'attentiveness to how one's actions get absorbed by the power/ knowledge regime' (1998: 360).

The ethical project for researchers takes as its starting point the right of all individuals to be included in mainstream education and focuses on the mechanisms which exclude individuals. There is, however, the risk of piety among researchers who stand on the sidelines and wax critical at teachers and others. The most important feature of the ethical project for researchers is that they acknowledge the way their own involvement in truth production excludes and disables individuals. This requires them to produce accounts of their research which have to be *'responded* to rather than just read' (Stronach and Maclure, 1997: 158, original emphasis). Booth (1998) argues plaintively that academics are too preoccupied to read each others' work, exchange ideas and reflect on their own research practice. Yet, his appearance in volumes on theorizing special education (Clark et al., 1998; Haug, 1998) and membership of an international research colloquium (Ballard, 1999; Booth and Ainscow, 1998b; Clark, Dyson and Millward, 1995) signals a move towards more self-conscious research practices and greater accountability among researchers. It is vital that researchers, regardless of the constraints under which they operate, subject themselves to their colleagues' critique. Booth dismisses Oliver's (1992b) contention that an earlier debate he had with Söder (1989; Booth, 1991) amounted to intellectual masturbation, claiming it 'had more to do with the macho politics of the locker room, professional self-interest and the termination of critique, than with the politics of disability' (1998: 85). This is to miss Oliver's point that such debate, without the involvement of disabled people, contributes little to understanding their experiences or changing their material circumstances and merely adds to their oppression. So, far from trying to engage in closure, Oliver was calling for a more meaningful debate about 'the terrain over which ideological struggles are being fought by disabled people in order to free themselves from the chains of oppression' (1992b: 26). Brantlinger has observed how several empiricist researchers have used ideology against inclusionists as a mechanism of closure, arguing that they would be on safer grounds if they branded them for 'idealism or demagoguery' (1997: 437). Yet, the notion of ideology is often misused or used vaguely to 'convey a sort of discredit. To describe a statement as ideological is very often an insult, so that this ascription itself becomes an instrument of symbolic domination' (Bourdieu and Eagleton, 1994: 266).

The under-theorized state of special educational practice (Slee, 1998) is being taken seriously by researchers and there have been many moves to remedy this. Recent theoretical developments include critiques of knowledge traditions within special education (Booth, 1998; Stangvik, 1998); engaging teachers in the theorizing process (Ainscow, 1998); and efforts to reconnect special education with educational theorizing more generally (Dyson, 1997; Slee, 1996). There have also been attempts to make greater use of imported theories (Skrtic, 1995; Slee, 1998) and this book has, of course, appropriated aspects of Foucault's methodology and analyses. The aim has not been to remain pure to Foucault, the very idea of which would have been abhorrent to someone who defied attempts to name his political perspective:

> I think I have in fact been situated in most of the squares on the political checkerboard, one after another and sometimes simultaneously: as anarchist, leftist, ostentatious or disguised Marxist, nihilist, explicit or secret anti-Marxist, technocrat in the service of Gaullism, new liberal, etc. . . . None of these descriptions is important by itself; taken together, on the other hand, they mean something. And I must admit that I rather like what they mean. (1984e: 383–4)

Instead, the intention has been to explore the relevance of his work to special education, discarding what is of no use. At a seminar on theorizing special education in Norway (Haug, 1998), some themes from this research were presented, following which the appointed critic suggested that Foucault would have 'celebrated' the arguments for a potential transgression of disabled identity, but would be 'a little shaken' by the analysis of the governmentality of mainstream peers. It was satisfying to have both pleased and disturbed Foucault. No doubt other Foucauldian scholars will find aspects of the application of his methodology and constructs to special needs troublesome, but the point has been to try to use Foucault's 'box of tools' (1977a: 208) critically, self-consciously and creatively, rather than faithfully, and to generate a response, whether negative or otherwise.

Theorizing, as Slee (1998) reminds us, is a political activity and Barnes (1996b) emphasizes the major role played by disabled people in politicizing disability:

> Since the politicisation of disability by the international disabled people's movement . . . a growing number of academics, many of whom are disabled people themselves, have reconceptualised disability as a complex and sophisticated form of social oppression (Oliver, 1986) or institutional discrimination on a par with sexism, heterosexism and racism . . . theoretical analysis has shifted from individuals and their impairments to disabling environments and hostile social attitudes. (Barnes, 1996b: 43)

Despite being the source of this 'gift', disabled people have been marginalized from research and knowledge production, through the unwillingness of researchers to alter research relations. Furthermore, they have been treated as objects of research, with researchers firmly in control.

> The social relations of research production provide the structure within which research is undertaken. These social relations are built upon a firm distinction between the researcher and the researched; upon a belief that it is the researchers who have specialist knowledge and skills; and that it is they who should decide what topics should be researched and be in control of the whole process of research production. (Oliver, 1992a: 102)

Ballard suggests that researchers' ignorance about disabled people leads them to 'establish a distance between themselves and those they study' (1997: 245) and construct them as 'other' (1997: 246). He calls for more explicit attempts to involve disabled people in research and analysing policy and practice as well as helping them to access resources and engage in political action in community groups. Armstrong, Armstrong and Barton (1998), argue for a greater attentiveness to the voice of those who have experienced discrimination, whereas Oliver (1992a) advocates privileging the voice of disabled people. Booth argues against this on the grounds that 'if special education or integration or inclusive education is concerned with all students rather than only disabled students, then disabled people cannot claim privileged status in understanding it' (1998: 85). Yet, if account is not taken of the subjugated position from which disabled adults, children and parents speak there is a danger that their voices will be silenced by more voluble speakers. Incitement to discourse, therefore, necessarily involves subversive research practices. Research involving disabled people can encounter problems, but these usually arise from structural, environmental or attitudinal barriers rather than from any limitations of the individuals concerned (Zarb, 1997).

Researchers' ethical work involves examining their own role in research and the effects of the kinds of knowledge about special education which they have produced. They might make themselves more available for criticism by colleagues and engage in 'experiment, creativity and risk' (Stronach and Maclure, 1997: 152). An example of this is a recent paper (Stronach and Allan, forthcoming) entitled 'Joking with disability: What's the difference between the comic and the tragic in disability discourses?', which risked accusations of pretentiousness, attempts to colonize disabled people's experiences and the charge of 'who do they think they are?' These criticisms were indeed made, but alongside a more positive engagement with the text by journal referees, one of whom described him/herself as a 'disabled person — an academic, but also sometimes a comedian'. The *performance* of the paper at a conference, aimed at disrupting the unitary and unified narrative that these events usually require was also deeply disturbing for all concerned but was a useful experiment in risk-taking. Researchers might also explore different forms of knowledge production as part of their theoretical work, involving, for example, the arts (Ballard, 1998; Heshusius, 1988), and work at changing research relations in order to involve disabled people more fully and effectively. These are demanding tasks for the researchers, given the pressures of performativity (Lyotard, 1984) in which research knowledge must have political acceptability. Researchers' ethical work requires them to transgress against these imperatives, whatever the risks involved.

Actively Seeking Inclusion: An Aesthetic Discourse of the Self

By bringing city centres to a standstill and by blockading telethons, disabled people have served notice that they will not tolerate exclusion and patronage. (Shakespeare et al., 1996: 186)

There is much to learn from the efforts of pupils with special needs to actively seek inclusion, by challenging the mechanisms which aimed to label and exclude them. There is also a great deal to learn from disabled adults' actions in tackling oppression and dismantling the barriers created by a disabling society. The emergence of a new aesthetic discourse of pride, beauty and the celebration of difference gives disabled people a political voice while at the same time avoids valorizing their voice at the margins (Ram, 1993; Singh, 1995). The aesthetic discourse necessarily deconstructs its own 'celebratory rhetoric of difference, diversity, heterogeneity and localisms' (Ram, 1993: 11), which risks becoming a tool of an 'assimilationist and universalist drive' (ibid.) and seeks to 'strategically deploy "difference" in order to make a political difference' (Singh, 1995: 197).

Corbett (1994) suggests that there are parallels between disability politics and gay pride, but as Zola points out, there are some difficulties associated with claiming pride in one's disability:

> With the rise of black power, a derogatory label became a rallying cry, 'Black is beautiful'. And when women saw their strength in numbers, they shouted 'Sisterhood is powerful'. But what about those with a chronic illness or disability? Could they yell, 'Long live cancer' 'Up with multiple sclerosis' 'I'm glad I had polio!' 'Don't you wish you were blind?' Thus the traditional reversing of the stigma will not so easily provide a basis for a common positive identity. (1993: 168)

This has not proved problematic for prize-winning essayist Mairs, whose description of herself as a 'cripple' is meant to provoke and discomfit non-disabled people:

> People — crippled or not — wince at the word cripple, as they do not at handicapped and disabled. Perhaps I want them to wince. I want them to see me as a tough customer, one to whom the fates/gods/viruses have not been kind, but who can face the brutal truth of her existence squarely. As a cripple I swagger. (1986: 9)

Writers such as Oliver (1992b) have advocated a reversal of the damaging anti-labelling philosophy, as a means of reclaiming the disability that has been denied (or *stolen* from) disabled people, whereas others have sought to repair their spoilt identities, through activities such as art, photography and dance (Hevey, 1993; Morrison and Finkelstein, 1992). As well as providing more positive representations of disabled people which 'speak against the slug-like portrayal they normally endure' (Hevey, 1992: 84), the arts can educate non-disabled people, by challenging notions of 'assumed dependency' (Morrison and Finkelstein, 1992: 127). Gabel argues that interpreting disability as having aesthetic meaning enables non-disabled people to appreciate experiences of disability, by facing the 'forceful gaze of the other with opposition, even defiance' (1998: 17). Steady Eddie, a comedian with cerebral palsy has attempted to confront non-disabled people with their own disablism in a performance, for example with an observation that when he saw a sign for a disabled toilet, he went off to find one that worked. His *Quantam Limp* show earned the wrath of both critics and disability groups for telling 'cripple gags' and being insufficiently political (O'Kelly, 1994) and proved too much for the douce folk of Tunbridge Wells, who voiced their disgust and cancelled the show. Bataille suggests that each of the arts comprise different kinds of 'unproductive expenditures' (1985: 118) which 'have no ends beyond themselves' (ibid.), with poetry the purest form, since it signifies 'creation by means of loss' (1985: 120). He argues that unproductive expenditures such as the arts have an important role in a society where most things are judged in terms of their utility and 'violent pleasure is seen as *pathological*' (1985: 116, original emphasis).

The Ethical Project of Inclusion: Actively Shaping Ourselves?

The final thoughts in this book attempt to undo the inevitable closure they represent, but seek to involve everyone in the ethical project of inclusion, stressing that we each have different kinds of work to do on ourselves. Pupils with special needs might analyse their own and others' knowledge about their disability and develop strategies with which they are comfortable. Mainstream pupils could work on their governmental regime, emphasizing its positive, rather than negative, aspects. Teachers and other professionals might become more alert to the desires of pupils with special needs, while schools could become more responsive to diversity and avoid disabling practices. Researchers might scrutinize their own involvement in knowledge production and make themselves more willing to be criticized. They might also work on theorizing and changing research relations in order to involve disabled people more fully and effectively. The ethical work for parents has not been specified here because of the importance of focusing on schools and research, but they too are included in the project. They might, for example, help their children to articulate their desires and ambitions beyond school and examine the impact of subjecting their children to the surveillance involved in formal assessment or fund-raising activities. The kind of ethical work which each of us might practise has been specified only as a starting point; clearly individuals need to determine their own self-knowledge and conduct if it is to have its own efficacy.

The ethical work we all have to do on ourselves is necessarily never complete, always in process, creating ourselves as 'relational, conjunctive and dynamic' subjects (Braidotti, 1997: 68). It involves learning to respect difference in others and 'knowing how to respond to others . . . how to "go on" with them in practice' (Shotter, 1997: 353). The ethical project of inclusion could be thought of as a Deleuzian project of becoming or of 'immanence' (Deleuze, 1997: 4), which Braidotti observes is also a politics of desire: 'the only possible way to undertake this process is to actually be attracted to change, to *want* it, the way one wants a lover — in the flesh' (1997: 70). Inclusion, then, is an ethical project of responsibility to ourselves and others, which is driven by an insatiable desire for more.

References

ABERCROMBIE, N., HILL, S. and TURNER, B. (1988) *The Penguin Dictionary of Sociology*, London: Penguin.

AINSCOW, M. (1991) 'Effective schools for all: An alternative approach to special needs education', in AINSCOW, M. (ed.) *Effective Schools for All*, London: David Fulton.

AINSCOW, M. (1998) 'Would it work in theory? Arguments for practitioner research and theorising in the special needs field', in CLARK, C., DYSON, A. and MILLWARD, A. (eds) *Theorising Special Education*, London: Routledge.

ALDERSON, P. and GOODEY, C. (1996) 'Research with disabled children: How useful is child-centred ethics?', *Children and Society*, **10**(2), pp. 106–16.

ALLAN, J. (1995) 'Pupils with special needs in mainstream schools: A Foucauldian analysis of discourses', Unpublished PhD thesis, University of Stirling.

ALLEN, B. (1998) 'Foucault and modern political philosophy', in MOSS, J. (ed.) *The Later Foucault*, London: Sage Publications.

ANZALDÚA, G. (1987) *Borderlands: The New Mestiza = La Frontera*, San Francisco, CA: Spinsters Ink/Aunt Lute.

APPLEBY, Y. (1994) 'Out in the margins', *Disability and Society*, **9**(1), pp. 19–32.

ARMSTRONG, D. (1995) *Power and Partnership in Education*, London: Routledge.

ARMSTRONG, D. and GALLOWAY, D. (1994) 'Special needs and problem behaviour: Making policy in the classroom', in RIDDELL, S. and BROWN, S. (eds) *Special Needs Policy in the 1990s: Warnock in the Market Place*, London: Routledge.

ARMSTRONG, D., ARMSTRONG, F. and BARTON, L. (1998) 'From theory to practice: Special education and the social relations of research production', in CLARK, C., DYSON, A. and MILLWARD, A. (eds) *Theorising Special Education*, London: Routledge.

ARMSTRONG, D., GALLOWAY, D. and TOMLINSON, S. (1993) 'Assessing special needs: The child's contribution', *British Educational Research Journal*, **19**(2), pp. 121–31.

ASCH, A. and FINE, M. (1997) 'Nurturance, sexuality and women with disabilities: The example of women and literature', in DAVIS, L. (ed.) *The Disability Studies Reader*, New York: Routledge.

ASHLEY, J. (1991) 'The silent house', in TAYLOR, G. and BISHOP, J. (1991) *Being Deaf: The Experience of Deafness*, London: The Open University.

BAILEY, M. (1993) 'Foucauldian feminism: Contesting bodies, sexuality and identity', in RAMAZANOGLU, C. (ed.) *Up Against Foucault: Explorations of Some Tensions Between Foucault and Feminism*, London: Routledge.

BALL, S. (1990a) *Politics and Policy Making in Education*, London: Routledge.

BALL, S. (1990b) 'Management as moral technology: A Luddite analysis', in BALL, S. (ed.) *Foucault and Education: Disciplines and Knowledge*, London: Routledge.

BALLARD, K. (1996) 'Inclusive education in New Zealand: Culture, context and ideology', *Cambridge Journal of Education*, **26**(1), pp. 33–45.

BALLARD, K. (1997) 'Researching disability and inclusive education: Participation, construction and interpretation', *International Journal of Inclusive Education*, **1**(3), pp. 243–56.

BALLARD, K. (ed.) (1999) *Inclusive Education: International Voices on Disability and Justice*, London: Falmer Press.

BARNES, C. (1996a) 'Visual impairment as disability', in HALES, G. (ed.) *Beyond Disability*, London: Sage/Open University Press.

BARNES, C. (1996b) 'Theories of disability and the origins of the oppression of disabled people in Western Society', in BARTON, L. (ed.) *Disability and Society: Emerging Issues and Insights*, London: Longman.

BARNES, C. and MERCER, G. (1997) 'Breaking the mould? An introduction to doing disability research', in BARNES, C. and MERCER, G. (eds) *Doing Disability Research*, Leeds: The Disability Press.

BARRON, K. (1997) 'The bumpy road to womanhood', *Disability and Society*, **12**(2), pp. 223–40.

BARTKY, S. (1988) 'Foucault, feminity and the modernisation of patriarchal power', in DIAMOND, I. and QUINBY, L. (eds) *Feminism and Foucault: Reflections on Resistance*, Boston, MA: Northeastern University Press.

BARTKY, S. (1990) *Femininity and Domination: Studies in the Phenomenlogy of Oppression*, London: Routledge.

BARTON, L. (1989) *Integration: Myth or Reality?* Lewes: The Falmer Press.

BARTON, L. (1993a) 'Labels, markets and inclusive education', in VISSER, J. and UPTON, G. (eds) *Special Education in Britain after Warnock*, London: David Fulton.

BARTON, L. (1993b) 'The struggle for citizenship: The case of disabled people', *Disability, Handicap and Society*, **8**(3), pp. 235–48.

BARTON, L. (1997) 'Inclusive education: Romantic, subversive or realistic?', *International Journal of Inclusive Education*, **1**(3), pp. 231–42.

BARTON, L. and CORBETT, J. (1993) 'Special needs in further education: The challenge of inclusive provision', *European Journal of Special Needs Education*, **8**(1), pp. 14–23.

BARTON, L. and LANDEMAN, M. (1993) 'The politics of integration: Observations on the Warnock Report', in SLEE, R. (ed.) *Is There a Desk with My Name on It? The Politics of Integration*, London: Falmer Press.

BARTON, L. and TOMLINSON, S. (1981) (eds) *Special Education: Policy, Practices and Social Issues*, London: Harper Row.

BARTON, L. and TOMLINSON, S. (1984) *Special Education and Social Interests*, Beckenham, Croom Helm.

BATAILLE, G. (1985) 'The notion of expenditure', in STOEKL, A. (ed.) *Georges Bataille, Visions of Excess: Selected Writings, 1927–1939*, Minneapolis, MN: University of Minnesota Press.

BAUMAN, Z. (1996) 'On communitarians and human freedom: Or how to square the circle', *Theory, Culture and Society*, **13**(2), pp. 79–90.

BENABIB, S. (1990) 'Epistemologies of postmodernism: A rejoinder to Jean-Francis Lyotard', in NICHOLSON, L. (ed.) *Feminism/Postmodernism*, London: Routledge.

BERLINER, W. (1993) 'Needs that are not being met', *The Guardian (Education)*, 25 May, p. 4.

BERMAN, M. (1982) *All That Is Solid Melts into Air: The Experience of Modernity*, New York, Simon and Schuster.

BERNAUR, J. (1988) 'Michel Foucault's "ecstatic thinking"', in BERNAUR, J. and RASMUSSEN, D. (eds) *The Final Foucault*, Cambridge, MA: MIT.

BHABHA, H. (1994) *The Location of Culture*, London: Routledge.

BIENVENUE, M. (1989) 'Disability', *The Bicultural Center News*, **13**, April, p. 1.

BINET, A. and SIMON, T. (1914) *Mentally Defective Children*, London: Edward Arnold.

BLACKER, D. (1998) 'Intellectuals at work and in power: Toward a Foucaultian research ethic', in POPEKEWITZ, T. and BRENNAN, M. (eds) *Foucault's Challenge: Discourse, Knowledge, and Power in Education*, New York: Teachers College Press.

BOOTH, T. (1988) 'Challenging conceptions of deafness', in BARTON, L. (ed.) *The Politics of Special Educational Needs*, London: Falmer Press.

BOOTH, T. (1991) 'Integration, disability and commitment: A response to Martin Söder', *European Journal of Special Needs Education*, **6**(1), pp. 1–15.

BOOTH, T. (1996) 'Stories of exclusion: Natural and unnatural selection', in BLYTH, E. and MILNER, J. (eds) *Exclusion from School: Inter-professional Issues for Policy and Practice*, London: Routledge.

BOOTH, T. (1998) 'The poverty of special education: Theories to the rescue?', in CLARK, C., DYSON, A. and MILLWARD, A. (eds) *Theorising Special Education*, London: Routledge.

BOOTH, T. and AINSCOW, M. (1998a) 'Scotland response: Professionals at the centre?', in BOOTH, T. and AINSCOW, M. (eds) *From Them to Us: An International Study of Inclusion in Education*, London: Routledge.

BOOTH, T. and AINSCOW, M. (1998b) (eds) *From Them to Us: An International Study of Inclusion in Education*, London: Routledge.

BOOTH, T. and BOOTH, W. (1996) 'Sounds of silence: Narrative research with inarticulate subjects', *Disability and Society*, **11**(1), pp. 55–69.

BORDIEU, P. and EAGLETON, T. (1994) 'Doxa and common life: An interview', in ZIZEK, S. (ed.) *Mapping Ideology*, New York: Verso.

BORDO, S. (1989) 'The body and the reproduction of feminity', in JAGGAR, A. and BORDO, S. (eds) *Gender/Body/Knowledge*, New Brunswick, NJ and London: Rutgers University Press.

BOYNE, R. (1990) *Foucault and Derrida: The Other Side of Reason*, London/New York: Routledge.

BRAIDOTTI, R. (1991) *Patterns of Dissonance: A Study of Women in Contemporary Philosophy*, Cambridge: Polity Press.

BRAIDOTTI, R. (1997) 'Meta(l)morphoses', *Theory, Culture and Society*, **14**(2), pp. 67–80.

BRANFIELD, F. (1998) 'What are you doing here? "non-disabled" people and the disability movement: A response to Robert F Drake', *Disability and Society*, **13**(1), pp. 143–4.

BRANNIGAN, J. (1996) 'Writing DeTermiNation: Reading death in(to) Irish National Identity', in BRANNIGAN, J., ROBBINS, R. and WOLFREYS, J. (eds) *Applying: To Derrida*, Basingstoke: Macmillan Press.

BRANTLINGER, E. (1997) 'Using ideology: Cases of nonrecognition of the politics of research and practice in special education', *Review of Educational Research*, **67**(4), pp. 425–59.

BRISENDEN, S. (1986) 'Independent living and the medical model of disability', *Disability, Handicap and Society*, **1**(1), pp. 173–8.

BRITZMAN, D. (1995) 'The question of belief: Writing poststructural ethnography', *Qualitative Studies in Education*, **8**(3), pp. 229–38.

BROWN, H. (1994) '"An ordinary sexual life?": A review of the normalisation principle as it applies to the sexual options of people with learning disabilities', *Disability and Society*, **9**(2), pp. 123–44.

BROWN, W. (1998) 'Genealogical politics', in MOSS, J. (ed.) *The Later Foucault*, London: Sage Publications.

BUTLER, J. (1990) *Gender Trouble: Feminism and the Subversion of Identity*, London: Routledge.

CASLING, D. (1993) 'Cobblers and song-birds: The language and imagery of disability', *Disability, Handicap and Society*, **8**(2), pp. 199–206.

CHERRYHOLMES, C. (1988) *Power and Criticism: Poststructural Investigations in Education*, New York: Teachers College Press.

CHESTON, R. (1994) 'The accounts of special education leavers', *Disability and Society*, **9**(1), pp. 59–69.

CHRISTIANSEN, J. and BARNARTT, S. (1995) *Deaf President Now! The 1988 Revolution at Gallaudet University*, Washington, DC: Gallaudet University Press.

CLARK, C., DYSON, A. and MILLWARD, A. (1995) (eds) *Towards Inclusive Schools?* London: David Fulton.

CLARK, C., DYSON, A. and MILLWARD, A. (1998) *Theorising Special Education*, London: Routledge.

CLARK, C., DYSON, A., MILLWARD, A. and SKIDMORE, D. (1997) *New Directions in Special Needs: Innovations in Mainstream Schools*, London: Cassell.

CLELLAND, A. and SUTHERLAND, E. (1996) *Children's Rights in Scotland*, Edinburgh: W Green/Sweet and Maxwell.

CLOUGH, P. (1995) 'Problems of identity and method in the investigation of special needs', in CLOUGH, P. and BARTON, L. (eds) *Making Difficulties: Research and the Construction of SEN*, London: Paul Chapman.

CLOUGH, P. and BARTON, L. (1995) (eds) *Making Difficulties: Research and the Construction of SEN*, London: Paul Chapman.

COLLINS, P. (1991) *Black Feminist Thought: Knowledge, Consciousness and the Politics of Empowerment*, New York: Routledge.

CONNELLY, W. (1998) 'Beyond good and evil: The ethical sensibility of Michel Foucault', in MOSS, J. (ed.) *The Later Foucault*, London: Sage.

COOPER, P. (1993) *Effective Schools for Disaffected Students: Integration and Segregation*, London: Routledge.

CORBETT, J. (1989) 'The quality of life in the "independence" curriculum', *Disability, Handicap and Society*, **4**(2), pp. 145–63.

CORBETT, J. (1993) 'Postmodernism and the "special needs" metaphors', *Oxford Review of Education*, **19**, pp. 547–53.

CORBETT, J. (1994) 'A proud label: Exploring the relationship between disability politics and gay pride', *Disability and Society*, **9**(3), pp. 343–57.

CORBETT, J. (1996) *Bad Mouthing: The Language of Special Needs*, London: Falmer Press.

CORBETT, J. (1997) 'Include/exclude: Redefining the boundaries', *International Journal of Inclusive Education*, **1**(1), pp. 55–64.

CORKER, M. (1993) 'Integration and deaf people: The policy and power of enabling environments', in SWAIN, J., FINKELSTEIN, V., FRENCH, S. and OLIVER, M. (eds) *Disabling Barriers — Enabling Environments*, London: Sage Publications/Open University Press.

CORKER, M. (1996a) 'A hearing difficulty as impairment', in HALES, G. (ed.) *Beyond Disability: Towards an Enabling Society*, London: Sage/Open University Press.

CORKER, M. (1996b) *Deaf Transitions: Images and Origins of Deaf Families, Deaf Communities and Deaf Identities*, London: Jessica Kingsley Publishers.

DAVIDSON, A. (1986) 'Archaeology, genealogy, ethics', in HOY, D. (ed.) *Foucault: A Critical Reader*, Oxford: Basil Blackwell.

DEAN, M. (1996) 'Foucault, government and the enfolding of authority', in BARRY, A., OSBORNE, T. and ROSE, N. (eds) *Foucault and Political Reason: Liberalism, Neoliberalism and Rationalities of Government*, London: UCL Press.

DELEUZE, G. (1988) *Foucault* (translated by S. HAND), Minneapolis, MN: University of Minnesota Press.

DELEUZE, G. (1997) 'Immanence: A life . . .' *Theory, Culture and Society*, **14**(2), pp. 3–7.

DELEUZE, G. and FOUCAULT, M. (1977) 'Intellectuals and power: A conversation between Michel Foucault and Giles Deleuze', in BOUCHARD, D. (ed.) *Michel Foucault, Language, Counter Memory, Practice: Selected Essays and Interviews*, New York: Cornell University Press.

DEPARTMENT FOR EDUCATION (DfE) (1994) *Code of Practice on the Identification and Assessment of Special Educational Needs*, London: DFE.

DEPARTMENT OF EDUCATION AND SCIENCE (DES) (1978) *Report of the Committee of Enquiry into the Education of Handicapped Children and Young People* (The Warnock report), London: HMSO.

DERRIDA, J. (1972) 'Plato's pharmacy', in *Dissemination*, translated by B. JOHNSON, Chicago, IL: University of Chicago Press.

DERRIDA, J. (1990) 'Some statements and truisms about neologisms, newisms, postisms, parasitisms and other small seisisms', in CARROL, D. (ed.) *The States of 'Theory': History, Art and Culture*, New York: Columbia Press.

DEVEUX, M. (1996) 'Feminism and empowerment: A critical reading of Foucault', in HEKMAN, S. (ed.) *Feminist Interpretations of Michel Foucault*, Pennsylvania, PA: Pennsylvania State University Press.

DIRKSEN, H., BAUMAN, L. and DRAKE, J. (1997) 'Silence is not without voice: Including deaf culture within multicultural curricula', in DAVIS, L. (ed.) *The Disability Studies Reader*, London/New York: Routledge.

DREYFUS, H. and RABINOW, P. (1982) *Michel Foucault: Beyond Structuralism and Hermeneutics*, Brighton: The Harvester Press.

DREYFUS, H. and RABINOW, P. (1986) 'What is maturity? Habermas and Foucault on "What is enlightenment?"' in HOY, D. (ed.) *Foucault: A Critical Reader*, Oxford: Basil Blackwell.

DYSON, A. (1997) 'Special and educational disadvantage: Reconnecting special needs education', *British Journal of Special Education*, **24**(4), pp. 152–7.

EVANS, J., LUNT, I., NORWICH, B., STEEDMAN, J. and WEDELL, K. (1994) 'Clusters: A collaborative approach to meeting special educational needs', RIDDELL, S. and BROWN, S. (eds) *Special Needs Policy in the 1990s: Warnock in the Market Place*, London: Routledge.

FAIRCLOUGH, N. (1992) *Discourse and Social Change*, Cambridge: Polity.

FELMAN, S. (1982) 'Psychoanalysis and teacher education: Teaching terminable and interminable', *Yale French Studies*, **63**, pp. 21–44.

FENDLER, L. (1998) 'What is it impossible to think? A genealogy of the educated subject', in POPKEWITZ, T. and BRENNAN, M. (eds) *Foucault's Challenge: Discourse, Knowledge and Power in Education*, New York: Teachers College Press.

FINGER, A. (1992) 'Forbidden fruit', *New Internationalist*, **233**, pp. 8–10.

FINKELSTEIN, V. (1980) *Attitudes and Disabled People*, New York: World Rehabilitation Fund.

FINKELSTEIN, V. (1990) 'We are not disabled, "you" are', in GREGORY, S. and HARTLEY, G. (eds) *Constructing Deafness*, London/Milton Keynes: Pinter/Open University Press.

FINKELSTEIN, V. (1993a) 'Disability: A social challenge or an administrative responsibility?', in SWAIN, J., FINKELSTEIN, V., FRENCH, S. and OLIVER, M. (eds) *Disabling Barriers — Enabling Environments*, London: Sage/Open University.

FINKELSTEIN, V. (1993b) *Workbook 1: Being Disabled*, K655, The Disabling Society, Buckingham: Open University Press.

FINKELSTEIN, V. (1996) 'Inside out', Unpublished discussion paper.

FISH, J. (1990) 'Sensitivity to special needs: Trends and prospects', in EVANS, P. and VARMA, V. (eds) *Special Education: Past, Present and Future*, Basingstoke: Falmer Press.

FLETCHER-CAMPBELL, F. with HALL, C. (1993) *LEA Support for Special Needs*, London: NFER-Nelson.

FOUCAULT, M. (1967) *Madness and Civilisation*, London: Tavistock.

FOUCAULT, M. (1971) 'Theories et institutions penales', *Annuaire du college de France 1971–72*.

FOUCAULT, M. (1972) *The Archaeology of Knowledge*, London: Tavistock.

FOUCAULT, M. (1973a) *The Order of Things: An Archaeology of the Human Sciences*, New York: Vintage.

FOUCAULT, M. (1973b) *The Birth of the Clinic*, London: Routledge.

FOUCAULT, M. (1976) *The History of Sexuality*, Harmondsworth: Penguin.

FOUCAULT, M. (1977a) 'Intellectuals and power: A conversation between Michel Foucault and Giles Deleuze', in BOUCHARD, D. (ed.) *Language, Counter-memory, Practice: Selected Essays and Interviews by Michel Foucault*, Oxford: Basil Blackwell.

FOUCAULT, M. (1977b) *Discipline and Punish*, London: Penguin.

FOUCAULT, M. (1977c) 'A preface to transgression', in BOUCHARD, D. (ed.) *Language, Counter-memory, Practice: Selected Essays and Interviews by Michel Foucault*, Oxford: Basil Blackwell.

FOUCAULT, M. (1977d) 'Theatrum philosophicum', in BOUCHARD, D. (ed.) *Language, Countermemory, Practice: Selected Essays and Interviews by Michel Foucault*, Oxford: Basil Blackwell.

FOUCAULT, M. (1980a) 'The confession of the flesh', in GORDON, C. (ed.) *Power/Knowledge: Selected Interviews and Other Writings 1972–1977*, Brighton: Harvester.

FOUCAULT, M. (1980b) 'The history of sexuality', in GORDON, C. (ed.) *Power/knowledge: Selected Interviews and Other Writings, 1972–77*, Brighton: Harvester.

FOUCAULT, M. (1982) 'The subject and power', in DREYFUS, H. and RABINOW, P. (eds) *Michel Foucault: Beyond Structuralism and Hermeneutics*, Brighton: Harvester.

FOUCAULT, M. (1984a) 'On the genealogy of ethics: An overview of work in progress', in RABINOW, P. (ed.) *The Foucault Reader*, Harmondsworth: Penguin.

FOUCAULT, M. (1984b) 'What is enlightenment?' in RABINOW, P. (ed.) *The Foucault Reader*, Harmondsworth: Penguin.

FOUCAULT, M. (1984c) 'Nietzsche, genealogy, history', in RABINOW, P. (ed.) *The Foucault Reader*, London: Peregrine.

FOUCAULT, M. (1984d) 'Sex, power and the politics of identity: An interview', *The Advocate*, **400**, pp. 26–58.

FOUCAULT, M. (1984e) 'Polemics, politics and problematization: An interview with Michel Foucault', in RABINOW, P. (ed.) *The Foucault Reader*, Harmondsworth: Penguin.

FOUCAULT, M. (1987a) 'The ethic of care for the self as a practice of freedom', *Philosophy and Social Criticism*, **12**, pp. 112–31.

FOUCAULT, M. (1987b) *The Use of Pleasure: The History of Sexuality*, **2**, (translated by R. HURLEY), Harmondsworth: Penguin.

FOUCAULT, M. (1988a) 'Technologies of the self', in MARTIN, L., GUTMAN, H. and HUTTON, P. (eds) *Technologies of the Self: A Seminar with Michel Foucault*, London: Tavistock.

FOUCAULT, M. (1988b) *The Care of the Self: The History of Sexuality*, **3**, (translated by R. HURLEY), New York: Routledge.

FOUCAULT, M. (1988c) 'The minimalist self', in KRITZMAN, L. (ed.) *Michel Foucault Politics, Philosophy, Culture: Interviews and Other Writings 1977–1984*, Oxford: Basil Blackwell.

FOUCAULT, M. (1988d) 'Politics and reason', in KRITZMAN, L. (ed.) *Michel Foucault Politics, Philosophy, Culture: Interviews and Other Writings 1977–1984*, Oxford: Basil Blackwell.

FOUCAULT, M. (1988e) 'Practicing criticism', in KRITZMAN, L. (ed.) *Michel Foucault: Politics, Philosophy, Culture*, New York: Routledge.

FOUCAULT, M. (1988f) 'The masked philosopher', in KRITZMAN, L. (ed.) *Michel Foucault: Politics, Philosophy, Culture*, New York: Routledge.

FOUCAULT, M. (1991a) 'Governmentality', in BURCHELL, G., GORDON, C. and MILLER, P. (eds) *The Foucault Effect: Studies in Governmentality*, Hemel Hempstead: Harvester Wheatsheaf.

FOUCAULT, M. (1991b) *Remarks on Marx: Conversations with Duccio Trombadori*, New York: Semiotext(e), Columbia University.

FRENCH, S. (1993a) 'Disability, impairment or something in between?' in SWAIN, J., FINKELSTEIN, V., FRENCH, S. and OLIVER, M. (eds) *Disabling Barriers — Enabling Environments*, London: Sage/Open University.

FRENCH, S. (1993b) 'What's so great about independence?', in SWAIN, J., FINKELSTEIN, V., FRENCH, S. and OLIVER, M. (eds) *Disabling Barriers — Enabling Environments*, London: Sage/Open University.

FULCHER, G. (1989) *Disabling Policies? A Comparative Approach to Education Policy and Disability*, London: Falmer Press.

FULCHER, G. (1995) 'Excommunicating the severely disabled: Struggles, policy and researching', in CLOUGH, P. and BARTON, L. (eds) *Making Difficulties: Research and the Construction of SEN*, London: Paul Chapman.

GABEL, S. (1998) 'A theory of an aesthetic of disability', paper presented to the American Educational Research Association Conference, San Diego, April.

GALLOWAY, D. and GOODWIN, C. (1987) *The Education of Disturbing Children: Pupils with Learning and Adjustment Difficulties*, New York: Longman.

GALLOWAY, D., ARMSTRONG, D. and TOMLINSON, S. (1994) *The Assessment of Special Educational Needs: Whose Problem?*, London: Longman.

GARFINKEL, H. (1967) *Studies in Ethnomethodology*, Englewood Cliffs, NJ: Prentice Hall.

GEARHEART, B., MULLEN, R. and GEARHEART, C. (1993) *Exceptional Individuals: An Introduction*, New York: Macmillan.

GERBER, D. (1990) 'Listening to disabled people: The problem of voice and authority in Robert B. Edgerton's *The Cloak of Competence*', *Disability and Society*, 5(1), pp. 3–22.

GERBER, M. (1996) 'Reforming special education: Beyond "inclusion"', in CHRISTENSEN, C. and RIZVI, F. (eds) *Disability and the Dilemmas of Education and Justice*, Buckingham: Open University Press.

GIBBONS, F. (1985) 'A social-psychological perspective on developmental disabilities', *Journal of Social and Clinical Psychology*, 3(4), pp. 391–404.

GIPPS, C., GROSS, H. and GOLDSTEIN, H. (1987) *Warnock's Eighteen Per Cent: Children with Special Needs in Primary Schools*, Lewes: Falmer Press.

GIROUX, H. (1988) *Teachers as Intellectuals: A Critical Pedagogy for Practical Learning*, South Hadley, MA: Bergin and Garvey.

GIROUX, H. (1992) 'The hope of radical education', in WEILER, K. and MITCHELL, C. (eds) *What Schools Can Do: Critical Pedagogy and Practice*, Albany, NY: State University of New York Press.

GOFFMAN, E. (1963) *Stigma: Notes on the Management of Spoiled Identity*, Harmondsworth: Pelican.

GOFFMAN, E. (1971) *Relations in Public*, Harmondsworth: Penguin.

GORDON, C. (1980) (ed.) *Power/knowledge: Selected Interviews and Other Writings, 1972–77*, Brighton: Harvester.

GORDON, C. (1991) 'Governmental rationality: An introduction', in BURCHELL, G., GORDON, C. and MILLER, P. (eds) *The Foucault Effect: Studies in Governmentality*, Hemel Hempstead: Harvester Wheatsheaf.

GREENE, M. (1978) *Landscapes of Learning*, New York: Teachers College Press.

GREGORY, S. (1993) 'The language and culture of deaf people: Implications for education', *Deafness*, **3**(9), pp. 4–11.

HABERMAS, J. (1986) 'Taking aim at the heart of the present', in HOY, D. (ed.) *Foucault: A Critical Reader*, Oxford: Basil Blackwell.

HAMILTON, D. (1996) 'Peddling feel-good fictions', *Forum*, **38**(2), pp. 54–56.

HARAWAY, D. (1991) *Simians, Cyborgs and Women: The Reinvention of Nature*, New York: Routledge.

HARTSOCK, N. (1990) 'Foucault on power: A theory for women?', in NICHOLSON, L. (ed.) *Feminism/postmodernism*, London: Routledge.

HARTSOCK, N. (1996) 'Postmodernism and political change: Issues for feminist theory', in HEKMAN, S. (ed.) *Feminist Interpretations of Michel Foucault*, Pennsylvania, PA: Pennsylvania State University Press.

HARVEY, D. and GREENWAY, A. (1984) 'The self-concept of physically handicapped children and their non-handicapped siblings: An empirical investigation', *Journal of Child Psychology and Psychiatry*, **25**(2), pp. 273–84.

HASLER, F. (1993) 'Developments in the disabled people's movement', in SWAIN, J., FINKELSTEIN, V., FRENCH, S. and OLIVER, M. (eds) *Disabling Barriers — Enabling Environments*, London: Sage/Open University.

HAUG, P. (1998) 'Norwegian special education: Development and status', in HAUG, P. and TØSSEBRO, J. (eds) *Theoretical Perspectives on Special Education*, Kristiansand, Norway: Norwegian Academic Press.

HEGARTY, S. (1982) 'Meeting special needs in the ordinary school', *Educational Research*, **24**(3), pp. 124–81.

HEGARTY, S. (1993) *Meeting Special Educational Needs in Ordinary Schools*, London: Cassell.

HEGARTY, S. and POCKLINGTON, K. (1981) *Educating Pupils with Special Needs in the Ordinary School*, Windsor: NFER Nelson.

HESHUSIUS, L. (1988) 'The arts, science and the study of exceptionality', *Exceptional Children*, **55**(1), pp. 60–5.

HEVEY, D. (1992) *The Creatures That Time Forgot: Photography and Disability Imagery*, London: Routledge.

HEVEY, D. (1993) 'The tragedy principle: Strategies for change in the representation of disabled people', in SWAIN, J., FINKELSTEIN, V., FRENCH, S. and OLIVER, M. (eds) *Disabling Barriers — Enabling Environments*, London: Sage/Open University.

HINSON, M. (1991) 'Aspects of coping with change', in HINSON, M. (ed.) *Teachers and Special Needs: Coping with Change*, Harlow: Longman.

HOFFMEISTER, R. (1996) 'Cross-cultural misinformation: What does special education say about deaf people?', *Disability and Society*, **11**(2), pp. 171–90.

HUGHES, B. and PATERSON, K. (1997) 'The social model of disability and the disappearing body: Towards a sociology of impairment', *Disability and Society*, **12**(3), pp. 325–40.

JACKSON, R. (1993) 'Disadvantaged by semantics', *Times Educational Supplement Scotland*, 6 August.

JOHNSTON, B. (1977) 'The frame of reference: Poe, Lacan, Derrida', *Yale French Studies*, **55/56**, pp. 457–505.

JONES, A. (1998) 'Pedagogical desires at the border: Absolution and difference in the university classroom', Paper presented to Winds of change: Women and the culture of the universities international conference, Sydney, Australia, July.

KALLIANES, V. and RUBENFIELD, P. (1997) 'Disabled women and reproductive rights', *Disability and Society*, **12**(2), pp. 203–22.

KAMUF, P. (1991) (ed.) *A Derrida Reader: Between the Blinds*, New York: Columbia University Press.

KELLY, U. (1997) *Schooling Desire: Literacy, Cultural Politics and Pedagogy*, New York: Routledge.

KIZILTAN, M., BAIN, W. and CANIZARES, M. (1990) 'Postmodern conditions: Rethinking public education', *Educational Theory*, **40**, pp. 351–69.

KUNDURA, M. (1986) *The Art of the Novel* (trans. L. ASHER), London: Faber and Faber.

KYLE, C. and DAVIES, K. (1991) 'Attitudes of mainstream pupils towards mental retardation: Pilot study at a Leeds secondary school', *British Journal of Special Education*, **18**(3), pp. 103–6.

KYLE, J. (1993) 'Integration of deaf students', *European Journal of Special Needs Education*, **8**(3), pp. 201–20.

LACAN, J. (1977) *Ecrits: A Selection*, London: Tavistock.

LADD, P. (1991) 'Making plans for Nigel: The erosion of identity by mainstreaming', in TAYLOR, G. and BISHOP, J. (eds) *Being Deaf: The Experience of Deafness*, London: Printer Publishers.

LANE, H. (1995) 'Constructions of deafness', *Disability and Society*, **10**(2), pp. 171–89.

LATHER, P. (1986) 'Research as praxis', *Harvard Educational Review*, **56**(3), pp. 257–77.

LATHER, P. (1993) 'Fertile obsession: Validity after poststructuralism', *The Sociological Quarterly*, **34**(4), pp. 673–93.

LATHER, P. (1996) 'Methodology as subversive repetition: Practices toward a feminist double science', Paper presented to the Annual Meeting of the American Educational Research Association, New York: April.

LATHER, P. (1998) 'Other scenes of research and learning: Poststructuralism, postcolonialism and psychoanalysis', Paper presented to the Annual Meeting of the American Educational Research Association, San Diego, April.

LE CARRÉ, J. (1986) *The Perfect Spy*, London: Hodder and Stoughton.

LEVINAS, E. (1987) *Time and the Other*, Pittsburgh, PA: Dusquesne University Press.

LEWIS, A. (1994) 'What Katy did: A case study in communication between a pupil with severe learning difficulties and non-disabled classmates', *British Journal of Special Education*, **21**(3), pp. 101–4.

LIGGET, H. (1988) 'Stars are not born: An interptetive approach to the politics of disability', *Disability, Handicap and Society*, **3**(3), pp. 263–75.

LLEWELLEN, R. (1983) 'Future health services — a challenge for disabled people', *Australian Rehabilitation Review*, **7**(4), pp. 24–31.

LLOYD, M. and THACKER, A. (1997) *The Impact of Michel Foucault on the Social Sciences and Humanities*, Basingstoke: Macmillan Press Ltd.

LONSDALE, S. (1990) *Women and Disability: The Experience of Physical Disability Among Women*, New York: St Martin's Press.

LORDE, A. (1982) *Sister Outsider: Essays and Speeches*, New York: Spinsters Ink.

References

LOWSON, D. (1994) 'Understanding professional thought disorder: A guide for service users and a challenge for professionals', *Asylum*, **8**(2), pp. 29–30.

LUNT, I. and EVANS, J. (1994) 'Dilemmas in special needs: Some effects of local management of schools', in RIDDELL, S. and BROWN, S. (eds) *Special Needs Policy in the 1990s: Warnock in the Market Place*, London: Routledge.

LYOTARD, J. (1984) *The Postmodern Condition: A Report on Knowledge* (trans. G. BENNINGTON and B. MASSUMI), Manchester: University of Manchester Press.

LYNAS, W. (1986a) 'Pupils' attitudes to integration', *British Journal of Special Education*, **13**(1), pp. 31–3.

LYNAS, W. (1986b) *Integrating the Handicapped into Ordinary Schools: A Study of Hearing-impaired Pupils*, London: Croom Helm.

MACCANNELL, D. and MACCANNELL, J. (1993) 'Violence, power and pleasure: A revisionist reading of Foucault from the victim perspective', in RAMAZANOGLU, C. (ed.) *Up Against Foucault: Explorations of Some Tensions between Foucault and Feminism*, London: Routledge.

MAGILL, K. (1997) 'Surveillance-free subjects', in LLOYD, M. and THACKER, A. (eds) *The Impact of Michel Foucault on the Social Sciences and Humanities*, Basingstoke: Macmillan Press.

MAIRS, N. (1986) 'On being a cripple', *Plaintext: Essays*, Tuscon, AZ: University of Arizona Press.

MARKS, G. (1994) '"Armed now with hope . . .": The construction of the subjectivity of students within integration', *Disability and Society*, **9**(1), pp. 71–84.

MARKS, G. (1996) 'Coming out as gendered adults: Gender, sexuality and disability', in CHRISTENSEN, C. and RIZVI, F. (eds) *Disability and the Dilemmas of Education and Justice*, Buckingham: Open University Press.

MARSHALL, J. (1989) 'Foucault and education', *Australian Journal of Education*, **33**(2), pp. 99–113.

MCLAREN, P. (1995) *Critical Pedagogy and Predatory Culture*, London: Routledge.

MCROBBIE, A. (1994) *Postmodernism and Popular Culture*, New York: Routledge.

MEGILL, A. (1979) 'Foucault, structuralism and the ends of history', *Journal of Modern History*, **51**, pp. 451–503.

MEGILL, A. (1985) *Prophets of Extremity: Nietzsche, Heidegger, Foucault, Derrida*, Berkeley, CA: University of California Press.

MEYER, J. and ROWAN, B. (1978) 'The structure of educational organizations', in MEYER, M. (ed.) *Environments and Organizations*, San Francisco, CA: Jossey-Bass.

MILLER, J. (1993) *The Passion of Michel Foucault*, London: Harper Collins.

MITTLER, P. (1985) 'Integration: The shadow and the substance', *Educational and Child Psychology*, **2**(3), pp. 8–22.

MITTLER, P. (1996) 'Preparing for self-advocacy', in CARPENTER, B., ASHDOWN, R. and BOVAIR, K. (eds) *Enabling Access: Effective Teaching and Learning for Pupils with Learning Difficulties*, London: David Fulton.

MOI, T. (1985) 'Power, sex and subjectivity: Feminist reflections on Foucault', *Paragraph*, **5**, pp. 95–102.

MORRIS, J. (1991) *Pride against Prejudice: Transforming Attitudes to Disability*, London: The Women's Press.

MORRIS, J. (1993) 'Feminism and disability', *Feminist Review*, **43**, pp. 57–70.

MORRISON, E. and FINKELSTEIN, V. (1992) 'Broken arts and cultural repair: The role of culture in the empowerment of disabled people', in SWAIN, J., FINKELSTEIN, V.,

FRENCH, S. and OLIVER, M. (eds) *Disabling Barriers — Enabling Environments*, London: Sage/Open University.

MURPHY, R. (1990) *The Body Silent*, New York: WW Norton.

NIETZSCHE, F. (1961) *Thus Spoke Zarathustra*. Harmondsworth: Penguin.

OLIVER, M. (1986) 'Social policy and disability: Some theoretical issues', *Disability, Handicap and Society*, **1**(1), pp. 5–18.

OLIVER, M. (1987) 'Re-defining disability: A challenge for research', *Research, Policy and Planning*, **5**(1), pp. 9–13.

OLIVER, M. (1988) 'The social and political context of educational policy: The case of special needs', in BARTON, L. (ed.) *The Politics of Special Educational Needs*, Basingstoke: Falmer Press.

OLIVER, M. (1989) 'If it wasn't so sad it would be funny', *Disability, Handicap and Society*, **4**(2), pp. 197–200.

OLIVER, M. (1990) *The Politics of Disablement*, Basingstoke: Macmillan.

OLIVER, M. (1992a) 'Changing the social relations of research production?', *Disability, Handicap and Society*, **7**(2), pp. 101–14.

OLIVER, M. (1992b) 'Intellectual masturbation: A rejoinder to Söder and Booth', *European Journal of Special Needs Education*, **7**(1), pp. 20–8.

OLIVER, M. (1996) *Understanding Disability: From Theory to Practice*, Basingstoke: Macmillan Press.

OLIVER, M. (1997) 'Emancipatory research: Realistic goal or impossible dream?', in BARNES, C. and MERCER, G. (eds) *Doing Disability Research*, Leeds: The Disability Press.

OLIVER, M. and ZARB, G. (1989) 'The politics of disability: A new approach', *Disability, Handicap and Society*, **4**(3), pp. 221–39.

OLWEUS, D. (1994) 'Bullying at school: Basic facts and effects of a school based intervention programme', *Journal of Child Psychology and Psychiatry*, **35**, pp. 1171–90.

O'KELLY, L. (1994) 'Ready, steady, Eddie', *The Observer*, 11 September.

OPIE, A. (1992) 'Qualitative research, appropriation of the "other" and empowerment', *Feminist Review*, **40**, pp. 221–39.

ORNER, M. (1998) 'School marks: Education, domination and female subjectivity', in POPKEWITZ, T. and BRENNAN, M. (eds) *Foucault's Challenge: Discourse, Knowledge, and Power in Education*, New York: Teachers College Press.

PAYNE, T. (1991) 'It's cold in the other room', *Support for Learning*, **6**(2), pp. 61–5.

PIGNATELLI, F. (1993) 'What can I do? Foucault on freedom and the question of teacher agency', *Educational Theory* **43**(4), pp. 411–32.

PLUMMER, K. (1995) *Telling Sexual Stories*, London: Routledge.

POSTER, M. (1984) *Foucault, Marxism and History*, Cambridge: Polity Press.

RABINOW, P. (1984) *The Foucault Reader*, Harmondsworth: Penguin.

RAM, K. (1993) 'Too "traditional" once again: Some poststructuralists on the aspirations of the immigrant/third world female subject', *Australian Feminist Studies*, **17**, pp. 5–28.

RAMASUT, A. and REYNOLDS, D. (1993) 'Developing effective whole school approaches to special educational needs: From school effectiveness theory to school development practice', in SLEE, R. (ed.) *Is There a Desk with My Name on It?* London: Falmer Press.

RAMAZANOGLU, C. (1993) (ed.) *Up Against Foucault: Explorations of Some Tensions Between Foucault and Feminism*, London: Routledge.

RANSOM, J. (1997) *Foucault's Discipline*, Durham, NC/London: Duke University Press.

RESNICK, M. and HUTTON, L. (1987) 'Resiliency among physically disabled adolescents', *Psychiatric Annals*, **9**(4), pp. 1–7.

REYNOLDS, D. (1995) 'Using school effectiveness knowledge for children with special needs — the problems and possibilities', in CLARK, C., DYSON, A. and MILLWARD, A. (eds) *Towards Inclusive Schools?* London: Fulton.

RIDDELL, S. and BROWN, S. (1994) (eds) *Special Needs Policy in the 1990s: Warnock in the Market Place*, London: Routledge.

RIDDELL, S., BROWN, S. and DUFFIELD, J. (1994) 'Conflicts of policies and models: The case of specific learning difficulties', in RIDDELL, S. and BROWN, S. (eds) *Special Needs Policy in the 1990s: Warnock in the Market Place*, London: Routledge.

RIDDELL, S., BROWN, S. and DUFFIELD, J. (1995) 'The ethics of policy-focused research in special educational needs', in CLOUGH, P. and BARTON, L. (eds) *Making Difficulties: Research and the Construction of SEN*, London: Paul Chapman.

RORTY, R. (1990) 'Foucault, Dewey, Nietzsche', *Raritan*, **9**, pp. 1–8.

ROTH, J. (1992) 'Of what help is he? A review of Foucault and education', *American Educational Research Journal*, **29**(4), pp. 683–94.

ROWAN, J. (1981) 'A dialectical paradigm for research', in REASON, P. and ROWAN, J. (eds) *Human Enquiry: A Sourcebook of New Paradigm Research*, Chichester: John Wiley.

RYAN, J. (1991) 'Observing and normalizing: Foucault, discipline and inequality in schooling', *The Journal of Educational Thought*, **25**(2), pp. 104–19.

SACKS, O. (1990) *Seeing Voices*, London: Picador.

SAID, E. (1986) 'Foucault and the imagination of power', in HOY, D. (ed.) *Foucault: A Critical Reader*, Oxford: Basil Blackwell.

SANDOW, S. (1993) *In Special Need*, London: Paul Chapman.

SAWICKI, J. (1988) 'Identity politics and sexual freedom', in DIAMOND, I. and QUINBY, L. (eds) *Feminism and Foucault: Reflections on Resistance*, Boston, MA: Northeastern University Press.

SAWICKI, J. (1996) 'Feminism, Foucault, and "subjects" of power and freedom', in HEKMAN, S. (ed.) *Feminist Interpretations of Michel Foucault*, University Park, PA: Pennsylvania State University Press.

SCHAAFSMA, D. (1998) 'Performing the self: Constructing written and curricular fictions', in POPKEWITZ, T. and BRENNAN, M. (eds) *Foucault's Challenge: Discourse, Knowledge and Power in Education*, New York: Teachers College Press.

SCHINDELE, R. (1985) 'Research methodology in special education: A framework approach to special problems and solutions', in HEGARTY, S. and EVANS, P. (eds) *Research and Evaluation Methods in Special Education*, Windsor: NFER-Nelson.

SCOTTISH OFFICE (1997) 'Provision for pupils with special educational needs, 1995 and 1996', *Statistical Bulletin*, Edn/D2/1997/11.

SCOTTISH OFFICE (1998) *Special Educational Needs in Scotland: A Discussion Paper*, Edinburgh: The Scottish Office.

SCOTTISH OFFICE EDUCATION AND INDUSTRY DEPARTMENT (SOEID) (1996) *Children and Young Persons with Special Educational Needs: Assessment and Recording*, Edinburgh: HMSO.

SHAKESPEARE, T. and WATSON, N. (1997) 'Defending the social model', *Disability and Society*, **12**(2), pp. 293–300.

SHAKESPEARE, T., GILLESPIE-SELLS, K. and DAVIES, D. (1996) *The Politics of Disability: Untold Desires*, London: Cassell.

SHAPIRO, J. (1981) 'Disability and the politics of consititutive rules', in ALBRECHT, G. (ed.) *Cross-national Rehabilitation Policies*, Beverly Hills, CA: Sage Publications.

SHAPIRO, J. (1993) *No Pity: People with Disabilities Forging a New Civil Rights Movement*, New York: Times Books.

SHARP, S. and THOMSON, D. (1997) 'The establishment of whole school policies', in LINDSAY, G. and THOMPSON, D. (eds) *Values into Practice in Special Education*, London: David Fulton.

SHELDON, D. (1991) 'How was it for you? Pupils', parents' and teachers' perspectives on integration', *British Journal of Special Education*, **18**(3), pp. 107–10.

SHILDRICK, M. and PRICE, I. (1996) 'Breaking the boundaries of the broken body', *Body and Society*, **2**(4), pp. 93–113.

SHOTTER, J. (1997) 'Dialogical realities: The ordinary, the everyday and other strange new worlds', *Journal for the Theory of Social Behaviour*, **27**(2/3), pp. 345–57.

SHUMWAY, D. (1989) *Michel Foucault*, Charlottesville, VA: University Press of Virginia.

SILVERMAN, K. (1996) *The Threshold of the Visible World*, New York: Routledge.

SIMONS, J. (1995) *Foucault and the Political*, London: Routledge.

SINASON, V. (1992) *Mental Handicap and the Human Condition: New Approaches from the Tavistock*, London: Free Association Books.

SINGH, P. (1995) 'Voicing the "Other", speaking for the "self", disrupting the metanarratives of educational theorizing with postructural feminism', in SMITH, K. and WEXLER, P. (eds) *After Postmodernism*, London: Falmer Press.

SKRTIC, T. (1995) (ed.) *Disability and Democracy: Reconstructing Special Education for Postmodernity*, New York: Teachers College Press.

SLEE, R. (1993) 'The politics of integration — new sites for old practices?' *Disability, Handicap and Society*, **8**(4), pp. 351–60.

SLEE, R. (1996) 'Disability, class and poverty: School structures and policing indentities', in CHRISTENSEN, C. and RIZVI, F. (eds) *Disability and the Dilemmas of Education and Justice*, Buckingham: Open University Press.

SLEE, R. (1998) 'The politics of theorising special education', in CLARK, C., DYSON, A. and MILLWARD, A. (eds) *Theorising Special Education*, London: Routledge.

SMART, B. (1986) 'The politics of truth and the problem of hegemony', in HOY, D. (ed.) *Foucault: A Critical Reader*, Oxford: Basil Blackwell.

SMART, B. (1998) 'Foucault, Levinas and the subject of responsibility', in MOSS, J. (ed.) *The Later Foucault*, London: Sage.

SÖDER, M. (1989) 'Disability as a social construct: The labelling approach revisited', *European Journal of Special Needs Education*, **4**(2), pp. 117–29.

SOPER, K. (1993) 'Productive contradictions', in RAMAZANOGLU, C. (ed.) *Up Against Foucault: Explorations of Some Tensions Between Foucault and Feminism*, London: Routledge.

SPIVAK, G. (1988) 'Can the subaltern speak?', in NELSON, C. and GROSSBERG, L. (eds) *Marxism and the Interpretation of Culture*, Basingstoke: Macmillan.

SPIVAK, G. (1994) 'Strategies of vigilence: An interview with Gayatri Chakravorty Spivak', in McROBBIE, A. *Postmodernism and Popular Culture*, New York: Routledge.

STALKER, K. (1998) 'Some ethical and methodological issues in research with people with learning difficulties', *Disability and Society*, **13**(1), pp. 5–20.

STANGVIK, G. (1998) 'Conflicting perspectives on learning disabilities', in CLARK, C., DYSON, A. and MILLWARD, A. (eds) *Theorising Special Education*, London: Routledge.

STONE, E. (1997) 'From the research notes of a foreign devil', in BARNES, C. and MERCER, G. (eds) *Doing Disability Research*, Leeds: The Disability Press.

STRATHCLYDE REGIONAL COUNCIL (1992) *Every Child Is Special*, Glasgow: Strathclyde Regional Council.

STRONACH, I. (1996) 'Fashioning post-modernism, finishing modernism: Tales from the fitting room', *British Educational Research Journal*, **22**(3), pp. 359–76.

STRONACH, I. and ALLAN, J. (forthcoming) '"Joking with disability" what's the difference between the comic and the tragic in disability discourses?' *Body and Society.*

STRONACH, I. and MACLURE, M. (1997) *Educational Research Undone: The Postmodern Embrace*, Buckingham: Open University Press.

STRONACH, I. and MORRIS, B. (1994) 'Polemical notes on educational evaluation in the age of "policy hysteria"', *Evaluation and Research in Education*, **8**(1 & 2), pp. 5–20.

SWAIN, J. (1993) 'Taught helplessness? Or a say for disabled students in schools', in SWAIN, J., FINKELSTEIN, V., FRENCH, S. and OLIVER, M. (eds) *Disabling Barriers — Enabling Environments*, London: Sage/Open University.

SWANN, W. (1983) 'Curriculum principles for integration', in BOOTH, T. and POTTS, P. (eds) *Integrating Special Education*, Oxford: Blackwell.

TAYLOR, C. (1984) 'Foucault on Freedom and Truth', *Political Theory*, **12**(2), pp. 152–83.

TAYLOR, G. and BISHOP, J. (1991) *Being Deaf: The Experience of Deafness*, London: Pintor.

THOMSON, R. (1997) 'Feminist theory, the body and the disabled figure', in DAVIS, L. (ed.) *The Disability Studies Reader*, New York: Routledge.

TOMLINSON, S. (1982) *A Sociology of Special Education*, London: Routledge and Kegan Paul.

TOMLINSON, S. (1996) 'Conflicts and dilemmas for professionals in special education', in CHRISTENSEN, C. and RIZVI, F. (eds) *Disability and the Dilemmas of Education and Justice*, Buckingham: Open University Press.

TROYNA, B. and VINCENT, C. (1996) 'The ideology of expertism: The framing of special education and racial equality policies in the local state', in CHRISTENSEN, C. and RIZVI, F. (eds) *Disability and the Dilemmas of Education and Justice*, Buckingham: Open University Press.

TURNER, B. (1984) *The Body and Society: Explorations in Social Theory*, Oxford: Basil Blackwell.

TURNER, V. (1969) *The Ritual Process*, London: Routledge and Kegan Paul.

UDITSKY, V. (1993) 'From integration to inclusion: The Canadian experience', in SLEE, R. (ed.) *Is There a Desk with My Name on It?* London: Falmer.

UNITED NATIONS (1989) *Convention on the Rights of the Child*, United Nations.

VISSER, J. (1993) 'A broad, balanced, relevant and differentiated curriculum?', in VISSER, J. and UPTON, G. (eds) *Special Education in Britain after Warnock*, London: David Fulton.

WALKERDINE, V. (1984) 'Developmental psychology and the child centred pedagogy', in HENRIQUES, J., HOLLWAY, W., URWIN, C., VENN, C. and WALKERDINE, V. (eds) *Changing the Subject: Psychology, Social Regulation and Subjectivity*, London: Methuen.

WALKERDINE, V. (1990) *Schoolgirl Fictions*, London: Verso.

WARD, A. (1990) *The Power to Act: The Development of Scots Law for Mentally Handicapped People*, Glasgow: Scottish Society for the Mentally Handicapped.

WARNOCK, M. (1991) 'Equality fifteen years on', *Oxford Review of Education*, **17**, pp. 145–54.

WARNOCK, M. (1992) 'Special case in need of reform', *The Observer*, 18 October.

WARNOCK, M. (1997) 'The keys to understanding: Interview with Baroness Warnock', *Special*, Spring.

WARREN, M. (1988) *Nietzsche and Political Thought*, Cambridge, MA: MIT Press.

WEDELL, K. (1990) 'Children with special needs: Past, present and future', in EVANS, P. and VARMA, V. (eds) *Special Education: Past, Present and Future*, Basingstoke: Falmer Press.

WOOD, S. and SHEARS, B. (1986) *Teaching Children with Severe Learning Difficulties: A Radical Approach*, London: Croom Helm.

WRIGHT, D. (1993) *Deafness: An Autobiography*, London: Penguin.

WYNTER, S. (1987) 'On disenchanting discourse: "minority" literary criticism and beyond', Cultural Critique, **7**, pp. 235–7.

YOUNG, I. (1990a) *Justice and the Politics of Difference*, Princeton, NJ: Princeton University Press.

YOUNG, I. (1990b) 'The ideal of community and the politics of difference', in NICHOLSON, L. (ed.) *Feminism/Postmodernism*, London: Routledge.

ZARB, G. (1997) 'Researching disabling barriers', in BARNES, C. and MERCER, C. (eds) *Doing Disability Research*, Leeds: The Disability Press.

ZOLA, I. (1993) 'Self, identity and the naming question: Reflections on the language of disability', *Social Science and Medicine*, **36**(2), pp. 167–73.

Index